Table of Contents

INTRODUCTION 1

CHAPTER ONE 4

THE WAY IT WAS, THE WAY IT IS 4

CHAPTER TWO 8

KNOW YOUR PURPOSE 8

CHAPTER THREE 12

PHILOSOPHY OF MINISTRY 12

DEVELOPING A PROPER THEOLOGICAL PHILOSOPHY 15
THE TWO SIDES OF GOD 16
CALLED TO BOTH 16

CHAPTER FOUR 18

THE PURPOSE OF THE CHURCH 18

PURPOSE ONE: FERVENT FELLOWSHIP WITH GOD 19
FERVENCY THROUGH PREACHING 21
PREACH THE WORD; LIVE THE WORD 24
THE MOTIVE OF PREACHING 26
PREACH POWERFUL, BOLD SERMONS 27
STRONG PREACHING ATTRACTS SINNERS 29
PREACHING HAS AN IMPACT 30
PREACHING AND COUNSELING 31
FERVENCY THROUGH PRAISE AND WORSHIP 33
FERVENCY THROUGH PRAYER 36

CHAPTER FIVE 39

THE SECOND PURPOSE OF THE CHURCH 39

To Be a Functional Family of God 39
Fellowship 39
Edification 42
A Test of Love 44
The Ability to Love 45

CHAPTER SIX 47

TO BE FISHERS OF MEN 47

Evangelism, the Door to the Church 48
A Bigger Picture of Evangelism 49

CHAPTER SEVEN 52

FACILITATING FULLY DEVOTED FOLLOWERS 52

Release into Meaningful Ministry 54
Developing Potential Leaders 56
Character Development 58

CHAPTER EIGHT 62

GOD'S AGENDA 62

God is the Initiator 65
Keeping His Own 65

CHAPTER NINE 67

THE PASTOR 67

THE TASK'S OF THE PASTOR	68
PERSONAL DEVELOPMENT	69
THE PASTOR AND RELATIONSHIPS	74
THE PASTOR IS A DEVELOPER OF PEOPLE	75
IS IT A JOB OR A MINISTRY?	76

CHAPTER TEN 78

THE MINISTRY OF THE SAINTS 78

EQUIPPED BY CHURCH LEADERSHIP	78
THE MINISTRY OF RESTORATION	79
THE SEQUENCE	80
MEANINGFUL SERVICE	81
YOUR BODY IS A TEMPLE OF THE HOLY SPIRIT	81
WHAT INFLUENCE ARE YOU MANIFESTING?	82
THE TENSION	83

CHAPTER ELEVEN 85

ORGANIZING FOR FULFILLMENT 85

A GIFT FOR THE CHURCH	85
THE NATURE OF THE CHURCH	86
BENEFITS OF EFFECTIVE ADMINISTRATION	88

BIBLIOGRAPHY 89

v

Introduction

The Great Awakening that occurred in the 1730's and 1740's formed much of the foundation of American democracy and individual freedom. A key figure in the midst of it was Jonathan Edwards. At the young age of 38, he preached his most famous sermon, "Sinners in the Hands of an Angry God." It sparked another wave of revival and shook the town of Enfield, CT. Today, there is only a rock with a memorial plaque covered by weeds and brush on the original property. Casual passersby would miss this historical treasure.

What happened to the influence of the Church in Enfield? Why did it fade away and become nothing but a historical landmark? Are current Church leaders effecting change upon our nation and the world in proportion to the effective influence that men like Jonathan Edwards, John Wesley and George Whitfield did? 21st Century Christian Leaders must face these questions as we develop ministries and move out in mission. It is God's plan that they perpetuate, not die.

According to W.E. Vine,

> "The mission of the church is to *preach* and *teach* the message of the *gospel* of Jesus Christ to the world, handing on the *tradition* of the faith.
>
> "*Preachers* and *teachers* are to teach sound *doctrine* and be able to *expound* the Word of God and give a *defense* of the faith, and to *admonish* when necessary. In addition to the *ministry* of preaching and teaching, other ministries given to the church are those of *apostle, prophet, evangelist, pastor,* and *helps*. In the *fellowship* of believers, however, all are called to *minister* and to make *intercessions*." [1]

In our search for answers, we must begin with the question, "Why does the Church exist? Is it a man made organization infringing upon the rights of individuals?" These are real questions asked by people. How will you answer them? The next question flows from the first; "what then are we to do?" I believe that leader's need to understand the Ministry and Mission of the Church so they can lead others into this understanding.

God has a purpose and a plan for individuals as well as His Church. By discovering these crucial aspects of successful ministry, we can effectively build them and they will perpetuate.

Joshua had this same concern as he approached his final days on earth. He knew the importance of successful transition of leadership having served as Moses' assistant in the wilderness and had learned what it would take to lead a great nation like Israel. With this in mind, he gathered the people of Israel together for his final charge to them as their leader. He began his discourse by reminding them of their history and how God had dealt with them. As he closed out his discourse, he gave them a challenge that has been quoted for thousands of years, *"And if it seems evil to you to serve the LORD, choose for yourselves this day whom you will serve, whether the gods which your fathers served that were on the other side of the River, or the gods of the Amorites, in whose land you dwell. But as for me and my house, we will serve the LORD"* Joshua 24:15 (The New King James Version 1982). "Joshua's noble decision for himself and his household has been an inspiration to succeeding generations of believers": **But as for me and my house, we will serve the Lord"** (Emphasis mine). (MACDONALD 1990)

So then, as with Joshua it must also be with leaders today; we must choose to follow Christ and instill His values in our families and the leaders with whom God has blessed us. Paul planned for his ministry to perpetuate through those who he personally trained. *"And the things that you have heard from me among many witnesses, commit these to faithful*

---

[1]W.E. Vine, *Vine's Complete Expository Dictionary Topic Finder.* (Nashville: Thomas Nelson, 1997, c1996)

men who will be able to teach others also" 2 Timothy 2:2 (The New King James Version 1982). As he wrote these words, he knew his end was near and execution awaited him. He had carried the torch of the gospel many years, and he is now concerned it should be handed on to others to carry it forward. Timothy must now take the lead, select, and instruct reliable men from among his people at Ephesus who are eligible to become another link in the chain of perpetuation by teaching the gospel to others.

Chapter One

The Way it Was, The Way it Is

Only when we compare the way things are to the way things were in the beginning of the Church can we answer the question, "Is this the way it's supposed to be?" This is a question on the minds of many followers of Christ. I believe there is much confusion surrounding the nature of the present day Church. To many, it seems the Church has separated from the Biblical revelation and they are seeking for what they call "the true Church." This is an elusive "Church" simply because people are seeking for some ideal that has been created in their own minds. The Bible reveals the nature of the Church as it operated in the power of the Holy Spirit and does not necessarily reveal a pattern of Church services and methodologies to copy.

The early Church was a living organism that manifested the love of Christ in such a way that even unbelievers were attracted to it. While sharing his passion for changing the world, Bill Hybels said, "Acts 2 tells us that this community of believers, this church, offered unbelievers a vision of life that was so beautiful it took their breath away. It was so bold, so creative, and so dynamic that they could not resist it. Verse 47 tells us the Lord added to their number daily those who were being saved" (Hybels 2009).

For the Church to be what it was, it must understand the origin, nature and function as revealed by Luke in the book of Acts. We cannot go back and repeat history, but we can use it as a reference point to get back on track.

During His earthly ministry, Jesus Christ prepared for the establishment of the church. He instructed His disciples with truth they did not fully comprehend, and He demonstrated for them life they did not fully appreciate at the time. In Matthew 16:18, he made an unfamiliar statement to His disciples, "And I also say to you that you are Peter, and on this rock I will build My church, and the gates of Hades shall not prevail against it" (The New King James Version 1982). "Here we have the first mention of the **church** in the Bible. It did not exist in the Old Testament. The church, still future when Jesus spoke these words, was formed on the Day of Pentecost and is composed of all true believers in Christ, both Jew and Gentile. A distinct society known as the body and bride of Christ, it has a unique heavenly calling and destiny" (MACDONALD 1990).

On the Day of Pentecost following the Ascension, Jesus poured out his Spirit upon those gathered waiting as He had commanded. This was the inauguration of the church. The baptism of the Spirit did something God had never done before in history; it united believers with Christ in a new relationship as fellow members of the spiritual body of Christ. "Before Pentecost, the Holy Spirit came upon men and dwelt **with** them. However, since Pentecost, when a man believes on the Lord Jesus, the Holy Spirit takes up His abode in that man's life forever (MACDONALD 1990). Believers shared the life of Christ in a way never before experienced. God united them with Him. The same Spirit of God that indwelt Jesus and the early Church now indwells us.

As to its nature, the church is one with Jesus Christ, sharing in His life. Paul said in Galatians 2:20, "I have been crucified with Christ; it is no longer I, who live, but Christ lives in me; and the life which I now live in the flesh I live by faith in the Son of God, who loved me and gave Himself for me (The New King James Version 1982). In the New Testament, Jesus Christ is presented as the Head of a new race. As Adam was the head of one race, Christ is the last Adam, the Head of a new race. Adam was the first man; Christ is the second man, the Head of a new race. As the First-born from the dead, Christ is the Head of a new race.

"The believer does not cease to live as a personality or as an individual. However, the one who is seen by God as having died is not the same one who lives. **It is no longer I who live, but Christ who lives in me**. The Savior did not die for me in order that I might go on living my life as I choose. He died for me so from now on He might be able to live His life in me" (MACDONALD 1990). The important factor here is yielding to the Holy Spirit in all things so the believer can be transformed into the image of Jesus Christ.

Christ is manifesting His life through those who have become partakers of His life by Holy Spirit baptism. Therefore, the nature of the church is one organic whole empowered by the life of Christ.

The third major revelation of the church that Acts gives us concerns the function of the church. The function of the church is to be the instrument of Jesus Christ, His hands, feet, and mouth, to carry out His will in the world. To understand the function we must answer the question, "What is the will of Christ?"

The will of God is the imparting of spiritual life where there is spiritual death. Jesus Christ ministers divine life through human instrumentality. That is the way it was and is to be.

The will of God is also the manifestation of light where there is darkness.

Third, the will of God is the production of love where there is apathy, bitterness, and hatred. Christ's love reaches through believers, His instruments, by the Holy Spirit. It produces in the believer love for the Lord, love for the brethren, and love for the world.

In summary, these are three great revelations of the church in Acts. As to its origin, Jesus Christ created it (Matt. 16:18). As to its nature, the church is one with Christ (1 Cor. 12:13). As to its function, the church is the instrument of Christ. Rom. 6:13 says, "Present yourselves to God . . . and your members as instruments of righteousness unto God."

Chapter Two

Know Your Purpose

(Colossians 1:9-12) ⁹ For this reason we also, since the day we heard it, do not cease to pray for you, and to ask that you may be filled with the knowledge of His will in all wisdom and spiritual understanding; ¹⁰ that you may walk worthy of the Lord, fully pleasing Him, being fruitful in every good work and increasing in the knowledge of God; ¹¹ strengthened with all might, according to His glorious power, for all patience and longsuffering with joy; ¹² giving thanks to the Father who has qualified us to be partakers of the inheritance of the saints in the light (The New King James Version 1982).

Choices! We make them every day. Career choices, life- mates, food on a menu, automobiles, and even where we will live. The list goes on and on. More important than the choice that is being made is the **motive** behind it. Most choices we make have to do with what we perceive as our right or what will make us the happiest.

When making choices, it is an essential part of the process to weigh them in the balance of purpose. Good things are not always the best things. Many people spend their lifetime doing good things for the Church and their communities; yet do not experience the fullness that Jesus said He came to give.

Another area of concern is the choice of friends. Do your friends have the same values as you? Are they enhancing your purpose or distracting you from it? Key relationships should complement and enhance your purpose. Furthermore, if you are still in the discovery stage of your God given purpose, the friends you associate with could actually take you away from God's ultimate best for you.

When I was young, I had a strong sense of a destiny in ministry. Unfortunately, the people around me did not have a clue about God given callings and destiny. There were even people close to me that were negative about my "calling." They could only see my immaturity at the time. They lacked the eyes of faith necessary to grasp the future. Because of this, I put the thoughts of serving God to the back of my mind.

As I grew older, I tried my hand at many different kinds of work trying to find fulfillment and purpose. I tried things like, restaurant work, automotive work, logging, door-to-door sales, electrical construction, and even tried my hand at being an insurance agent. As you can see, I had a variety of experiences. Yet, I was left with a feeling of missing something! That something was the primary purpose for which I was born; to serve Jesus and His Church as a Leader and a Teacher.

For me, it took a series of events, many of which were hard times, to bring me to a place where the people in my life actually supported my call and I could see more clearly God's purpose. To this day, I am sure, many of my old acquaintances still wonder!

A key to success in ministry is a proper attitude toward your purpose. The purpose of humanity is found in Christ. Consider the following passage:

Colossians 1:15-18 (The Message) *We look at this Son and see the God who cannot be seen. We look at this Son and see God's original purpose in everything created. For everything, absolutely everything, above and below, visible and invisible, rank after rank after rank of angels— everything got started in him and finds its purpose in him. He was there before any of it came into existence and holds it all together right up to this moment. And when it comes to the church, he organizes and holds it together, like a head does a body.* (Peterson Copyright © 1993, 1994, 1995, 1996, 2000, 2001, 2002)

Meditate on this passage. Let it get deep into your spirit. The closer you get to Jesus, the clearer your purpose will become! What Jesus did, we are to do; what Jesus said, we are to say. We are to be imitators of Him. Simply put, our purpose is to be Christ-like in character and conduct as well as leading others into this revolutionary experience. Remember, it is not about you. Jesus is the main thing. Keep the main thing, the main thing.

Finding Your Specific Purpose

I have had more people sit with me in counseling that could not grasp what their specific calling in the kingdom was. While there are no easy answers, there are answers! Be careful about people just telling you what they think you want to hear.

The first step is to identify the burden of your heart. As a young Christian, I was troubled by the lack of clear Biblical understanding amongst fellow believers. They did not talk about what they believed; they would talk about what the Church, as an institution believed. In discussions with cult members, most Christians were left confused, dazed and unsure of their own salvation! This was troubling to me. After my first encounter with a cult member, I realized I had to get into the Word, memorize it, and understand it.

The burden of my heart had been revealed. I saw a lack of Biblical understanding and wanted to do something about it. This, of course, started me on a journey that has brought me to the place of establishing Christian Schools, Ministry Schools and a Leadership Institute. At present, I am pioneering the Leadership Institute of New England as a part of a regional vision of equipping saints for the work of ministry (see Eph. 4:11).

Second, your purpose will be revealed as you give your life over to the Lord. The principal of this is found in Paul's letter to the Roman Christian's: *Romans 12:1-2 (NKJV)*[1] *I beseech you therefore, brethren, by the mercies of God, that you present your bodies a living sacrifice, holy, acceptable to God, which is your reasonable service. ² And do not be conformed to this world, but be transformed by the renewing of your mind, that you may prove what is that good and acceptable and perfect will of God.* (The New King James Version 1982)

The path to discovering the perfect will of God begins with self-sacrifice and is carried on with the process of transformation. You cannot effectively just add new beliefs to your life; you must remove the old, traditional beliefs that do not line up with the Word of God. That may even require a change of Church membership. If the Church you are in does not embrace Biblical doctrine, you are going to put your soul into a spiritual conflict with the teachers and leaders of that institution. Unless you are Biblically perceptive, you are not going to make headway; you will end up frustrating and alienating yourself from the very people you may help in the future. Do not be in a hurry! Enjoy the process of transformation. After all, it is only going to take a lifetime!

The third and final thing I will share with you is seek godly counsel. Do you have a mentor? Seek out godly men and women and find the one God ordains to mentor you as you prepare to fulfill your ultimate destiny.

Successful people do not hang around people who fail and have bad attitudes. Not all people fail because of bad attitudes. Life has its share of failures. The one's to follow are the ones who get back up after a failure and press forward with great resolve.

If the people you are associated with really do not care about you, find new friends. If your Pastor does not have a vision for releasing people into their gifts and callings, find a new Pastor! Make the sacrifice necessary to be in the perfect will of God.

Chapter Three

Philosophy of Ministry

Before we begin, we must answer the question, "What is philosophy as it relates to the Church?" According to the Encarta Dictionary, one of the definitions of philosophy is "a precept, or set of precepts, beliefs, principles, or aims, underlying somebody's practice or conduct." In essence, it is your viewpoint or worldview and how it pertains to the Church and its place in the world.

Everyone has a worldview whether they recognize it or not. In the broadest sense, a worldview is the standard by which an individual, knowingly and reflexively, interprets *all* information to sustain a dependable and sound understanding of the *whole* of reality.

A worldview acts like a fine filter in that it screens and analyzes and categorizes all information so we can make sense out of the world. It is the point of reference from which we discern fact from fiction, make cogent decisions, and formulate moral and spiritual standards.

Worldviews are made up of certain *presuppositions* that an individual believes to be true. These presuppositions form the outline of all worldviews. For example, Christians hold to the presuppositions the supernatural realm exists, God can be and wants to be known, Jesus is fully God and fully human, an heaven awaits us. These and a host of other beliefs are relevant to how Christians view religious, ethical, and other truths.

The most important factor to understanding the role of presuppositions in worldviews is they are assumed. They are rarely defended, discussed, or analyzed because everyone who accepts them thinks they are necessarily true. And indeed, in the minds of individuals, they *must* be true if a worldview is to accurately reveal truth as it in reality exists.

A worldview determines what reality to an individual or culture is. Supposed truth is largely determined by our worldview presuppositions. This is why, given the same data, people with different worldviews reach different conclusions. A worldview is similar to a set of colored glasses. If one looks at the same object through blue-colored glasses he will see it as blue, while another looking at the same object through orange glasses will see it as orange. This is why people with different worldviews will often see the same facts in a very different way.

In consideration of the effect of presuppositions, it is essential that one's philosophy flow from one's theology, that is, the study or the knowledge of God. Anyone who has ever asked the question "is there a God?" has entered into the field of theology. From the preschool aged Sunday school student to the postgraduate student in seminary, theology is being developed, defined and disseminated. Theology therefore becomes the starting point of developing effective ministry to the Church and mission to the world.

The Apostle Paul could arguably be called one of history's greatest theologians, second only to Jesus Christ. An example of His philosophy of ministry can be found in 2 Corinthians 2:14-6:10. His initial view is God is the source of all victory and accomplishments in the course of a believer's life, "*Now thanks be to God who always leads us in triumph through Christ, and through us diffuses the fragrance of His knowledge in every place*" (2 Corinthians 2:14, NKJV).

Although everyone has a theology, not all theology is correct. Theology must be based on the Word of God first. An unbiblical theology will result in an improper, dysfunctional ministry. Jay Adams aptly put it this way, "The fact of the matter is that it is irresponsible and dangerous to do practical work apart from a sound theological base. The only proper basis for Christian living and pastoral ministry is biblical and theological." (Adams 1974, 1975)

If Philosophy is divorced from theology, truth and facts become irrelevant. Relativism, the belief that concepts such as right and wrong, goodness and badness, or truth and falsehood are not absolute but change from culture to culture and situation to situation, become acceptable. If the Bible is not our source for absolute truth and the development of our theology, and personal experience is allowed to define and interpret what truth actually is, a saving faith in Jesus Christ is rendered meaningless.

Even across religious denominations and Christian Fellowships, the need for a consistent theology cries out. Erroneous beliefs based upon personal desires and preferences have created a chasm not only between denominations, but also within local churches. Because belief systems create ministry emphasis, a balanced, Biblical theology and ministry will result in the fulfillment of the purpose of the Church.

The Bible reveals the value, heart, character and purposes of God the Creator. *"Your word is a lamp to my feet and a light to my path."* (Psalm 119:105, NKJV) Because we live in a world that offers many opinions and worldly values it is comforting and assuring to know that the Scriptures give us the information we need to determine God's will.

When all is said and done, the only thing that matters is what God says, thinks, feels and mandates.

Allow the Word of God to shape your theology and philosophy of ministry. Stay true to the Biblical revelation and take away any function driven by faulty theology and traditions of men that are not producing results according to Biblical revelation.

Developing a Proper Theological Philosophy

Where do we begin? We start with the question "Who is God?" From there, we ask, "Who shall I be and what shall I do?" The purposes of the individual Christian and the corporate body of the Church originate from the unchanging character of God.

You should understand, as your revelation of God broadens and deepens, your philosophy of ministry would also change. Do not keep doing what you are doing just for the sake of protecting tradition. Often those that decry the fallacy of human traditions eventually create their own and spend their lives defending them. Jesus condemned the Pharisees for this very attitude, *"He said to them, "All too well you reject the commandment of God, that you may keep your tradition. For Moses said, 'Honor your father and your mother'; and, 'He who curses father or mother, let him be put to death.' But you say, 'If a man says to his father or mother, "Whatever profit you might have received from me is Corban"—' (that is, a gift to God), then you no longer let him do anything for his father or his mother, making the word of God of no effect through your tradition which you have handed down. And many such things you do." "* (Mark 7:9–13, NKJV)

As philosophy of ministry is developed, you may need to add to or even remove programs from your ministry. Some programs may no longer fit within the context of Biblical revelation. Annual reviews with ministry leaders can be helpful in determining functional success of ministries as well as determining essential changes that may need to be made. In my experience, I have seen that reducing the frequency of meetings actually increased the effectiveness. In essence, this philosophy is "less is more!"

The world is filled with religious organizations that continue to practice their faith in the old, traditional ways without embracing the fresh, relevant moves of the Holy Spirit. Many of them have seen serious decline in membership and are struggling to survive. For some of them getting a fresh perspective on their relevance and a willingness to embrace God's mandated purposes as revealed in the Bible will bring about a revival. If you are faithful to Biblical Theology and Philosophy, you will have nothing to be ashamed of at Jesus' return.

The Two Sides of God

At first, I am sure that the above subtitle has alarmed you. I am not referring to God having a split personality. I am talking about two aspects of His character; He is both a people oriented God and a Task oriented God. These two aspects of His character work in perfect harmony and God does not emphasize one over the other.

John 3:16 (NKJV) for God so loved the world that He gave His only begotten Son, that whoever believes in Him should not perish but have everlasting life. In this one verse, we have an illustration of both sides of God. The people oriented side of God is revealed in that He "loved" the world, even though the world He created did not love Him. The task-oriented side is revealed in the fact that He gave His only Son.

Love is best defined here as "the accurate estimate and adequate supply of another person's needs." God accurately estimated the need of a Savior for fallen man; then, His task-oriented side adequately provided Jesus and gave Him His mission in the earth.

Called to Both

God has called His Church to both relationships and work. This often creates a tension in Christian's as they seek to maintain a balanced life. People have a tendency to emphasize one more than the other does. To build a healthy, vibrant Church requires maintaining a stable balance between the task and relationship with God and one-another. Leaders have to be constantly re-evaluating their relationships and work.

Adjustments must be made based on a fair self-analysis. This often requires input from unbiased individuals. You do not need "yes men" surrounding you. You need people who can hear from God and love you enough to tell you the truth.

If you work alone in ministry, then you need to develop an accountability system with other seasoned ministry veterans. If you have a ministry team, then practice the habit of regular meetings for the purpose of healthy self-examination. Two extremes are often practiced in self-evaluation; passivity and being over-critical and self-condemning. If competent, honest, God-fearing individuals surround you then you have the opportunity for developing your God given gifts and fulfilling your purposes.

This is not an exclusive practice for people in leadership positions. All Christians need to practice healthy self-examination. An effective means to accomplish this is to be plugged in to small groups and develop healthy relationships.

In the next chapter, we will look at the Four Purposes of the Church based on the Scriptures.

Chapter Four

The Purpose of the Church

The purpose of the Church can be summed up in four categories that are derived from the two Greatest Commandments (Matt. 22:37-40) and the Great Commission (Matt. 28:18-20). The primary mission of the Church is declared in "The Great Commission," which Jesus gave to the Apostles before His Ascension. A form of the commission is found in all four Gospels and in the book of Acts, each writer reporting only a selected part of the total commission.

Matthew 22:37-40 (NKJV) [37] Jesus said to him, 'You shall love the Lord your God with all your heart, with all your soul, and with your entire mind.' [38] This is the first and great commandment. [39] And the second is like it: 'You shall love your neighbor as yourself.' [40] On these two commandments hang all the Law and the Prophets."

Matthew 28:17-28 (NKJV) [17] When they saw Him, they worshiped Him; but some doubted. [18] And Jesus came and spoke to them, saying, "All authority has been given to Me in heaven and on earth. [19] Go therefore and make disciples of all the nations, baptizing them in the name of the Father and of the Son and of the Holy Spirit, [20] teaching them to observe all things that I have commanded you; and lo, I am with you always, even to the end of the age." Amen. (The New King James Version 1982)

I am presenting a four-fold purpose paradigm to help Churches find purpose and accomplish what God intends. These are the four purposes as derived from these two passages:

1. To have Fervent Fellowship with God

2. To be a Functional Family of God

3. To be Fishers of Men

4. To Facilitate Fully Devoted Followers of Jesus Christ

Purpose One: Fervent Fellowship with God

Have you ever desired to have a passionate relationship with God? Fervency is having a keen enthusiasm or intense desire for something. We can be passionate about our favorite hobbies, food and movies. This same kind of passion can be transferred to our relationship with God. Fervency characterized Jesus' agony in Gethsemane, where his sweat fell to the ground as droplets of blood. Fervency describes Jacob's all-night wrestling match with the angel at Peniel.

In response to the question, "What is the greatest commandment?" Jesus declared, *'You shall love the Lord your God with all your heart, with all your soul, and with your entire mind.' 38 This is the first and great commandment. Matt. 22:37-38* (The New King James Version 1982). Our primary obligation is to love God with our whole being. That means we hold nothing back from Him! Do you love God that way? It is difficult to even fathom the idea. This means we must be growing in our love for God daily, moment by moment. The only person who has ever been able to love God in this manner is Jesus Christ. All of our efforts fall short of achieving this high and lofty goal. What do we do? Hide ourselves in Jesus and allow Him to love our Father through us.

The heart speaks of the emotional nature, the soul of the volitional nature, the mind of the intellectual nature, and strength of the physical nature. The motive for loving God this way is His love for us. Jesus declared God's love for mankind in John 3:16 "For God so loved the world that He gave His only begotten Son, that whoever believes in Him should not perish but have everlasting life." (The New King James Version 1982)

This passage gives us the most powerful definition of love: the accurate estimate and adequate supply of another person's need: God accurately estimated man's need of a Savior; the adequate supply: He adequately supplied a Savior in Jesus Christ.

Serving in ministry without loving God makes that person a modern day Pharisee. Allow God access to your heart and let Him bring healing and deliverance into your life so you can grow in loving Him.

Fellowship with God is carried out in two areas of our lives, our personal, private lives that are lived out before God and our corporate life, which is lived out in the midst of our fellow Christians. A personal relationship with God can develop a sense of well-being and a positive outlook concerning trials and tribulations and will be evidenced by our attitude toward fellow believers. In essence, our love for God affects our attitude and conduct toward fellow believers *"Beloved, let us love one another, for love is of God; and everyone who loves is born of God and knows God. He who does not love does not know God, for God is love. "* (1 John 4:7–8,) *"Beloved, if God so loved us, we also ought to love one another."* (1 John 4:11,) (The New King James Version 1982) When people respond in love to each other, they cover over the sins, or offenses, that would otherwise come between them *"Hatred stirs up strife, But love covers all sins."* (Proverbs 10:12) (The New King James Version 1982)

Fellowship, simply put, is sharing of common interests, goals, experiences or views. The Greeks used the word, "κοινωνία (*koinōnia*)" which referred to a close, mutual association with someone. Consequently, fellowship with God will require us to understand His views and vision. Again, this has to come from a clearly defined Theology derived from the Scriptures.

Fellowship with God further implies a friendship. , "You are as close to

God as you choose to be." (R. Warren 2002) This implies the only barrier to a fulfilled, meaningful relationship with God is you. A factor in the development of this friendship is complete honesty. We must learn to express exactly how we feel; this includes the positive feelings as well as the negative. Some of the Bible's greatest characters had moments of anger and disappointment with God. Because God loves us, He allows us to be expressive so He can heal us and give us a new perspective.

If we allow bitterness to grow in our hearts, our relationship with God will be diminished greatly. To overcome bitterness, a believer must first mature and understand God doesn't cause all the bad things to happen but He is at work despite them causing all things to work out for our complete good and edification *"And we know that God causes everything to work together for the good of those who love God and are called according to his purpose for them."* (Romans 8:28, NLT)

"Come close to God, and God will come close to you. Wash your hands, you sinners; purify your hearts, for your loyalty is divided between God and the world." (James 4:8, NLT) This is another promise from the Bible that assures believers of the reward of diligently seeking after God. We must realize God desires a relationship with us and wants us to know Him. He is not hiding from those that truly are seeking Him.

Fervent fellowship with God is developed and expressed primarily through three functions: preaching, worship and gifts of the Holy Spirit.

Fervency through Preaching

Fervent preaching can produce fervent disciples. A preacher who is passionate about God and spiritual realities will eventually rub off on others. Passion is contagious. The Book of Acts describes the first Christian community. Close fellowship, fervent preaching, earnest prayer, and evangelistic outreach marked it.

Passion is not a replacement for knowledge. Paul wrote to the Corinthian believers about zealous Jews, *"For I bear them witness that they have a zeal for God, but not according to knowledge."* (Romans 10:2) (The New King James Version 1982). Lack of the knowledge of God has done more damage to people and their view of life causing them to turn to rituals as a means of a sense of pleasing God. Unfortunately, some people have inoculated themselves against being passionate in addition to lacking knowledge.

John the Baptist was a fervent preacher. He was so passionate about what he was doing he cried out to the people calling them to repent and follow God with their whole hearts. *(John 1:15 NKJV) John bore witness of Him and cried out, saying, "This was He of whom I said, 'He who comes after me is preferred before me, for He was before me.' "*

The Apostle Paul was a man who preached with great passion (1 Thessalonians 1:5) "For our gospel did not come to you in word only, but also in power, and in the Holy Spirit and in much assurance, as you know what kind of men we were among you for your sake." (The New King James Version 1982) "By our gospel Paul does not imply a different message from that of the other apostles. The contents were the same; the difference was in the messengers." (MACDONALD 1990)

Preaching and teaching are a serious matter to be undertaken and preparation is necessary for it to be fruitful. The pastor, while following in the footsteps of Jesus, must be extremely diligent and apply himself to a lifetime of study.

In addition to this, he must allow his own personality to be used by the Holy Spirit in the delivering of his teaching and preaching. God has uniquely equipped each person and has selected him or her for the region they are in. They have been given a great opportunity by the Lord to stand out in their calling and cause great glory to be given to Jesus.

Strong preaching will affect the attitude of its listeners. The attitude of believers should be characterized by their single-minded desire and aim to fully please God and be zealous for His honor. As a result, believers will willingly and with great joy offer their bodies to God for his service. Romans 12:1 "I beseech you therefore, brethren, by the mercies of God, that you present your bodies a living sacrifice, holy, acceptable to God, which is your reasonable service." Proverbs 23:17 "Do not let your heart envy sinners, But be zealous for the fear of the LORD all the day;" (The New King James Version 1982)

Being single-minded as a Christian will help you to be effective. Paul was a man that experienced the fulfillment of God's purposes. He found joy in the midst of the most uncomfortable circumstances you could imagine. His focus was not on self, it was on God and pleasing Him alone. By focusing on God, His character, and His power, you will be able to bring the reality of His presence to a world that so greatly needs to yield to Him.

The contrast to single mindedness is double mindedness. James refers to the double-minded man as being unstable in all his ways (James 1:8) "he is a double-minded man, unstable in all his ways." If a person one day is optimistic and the next day pessimistic, they are the epitome of double mindedness. According to Vines double minded is, "dipsuchos (δίψυχος, 1374) which literally means "two-souled" hence, "double-minded" (Vine 1997, c1996)

A person who wavers is also living in two philosophical worlds. While he may reject the natural intellectually, he does not wholly commit to the supernatural. He is not a "one hundred per- center." Matthew 6:24 "No one can serve two masters; for either he will hate the one and love the other, or else he will be loyal to the one and despise the other. You cannot serve God and mammon. (The New King James Version 1982) The impossibility of living for God and for money is stated here in terms of masters and slaves. No one can serve two masters. One will inevitably take precedence in his loyalty and obedience. So it is with God and mammon. They present rival claims and a choice must be made. Either we must put God first and reject the rule of materialism or we must live for temporal things and refuse God's claim on our lives. (MACDONALD 1990)

As a Pastor, I have had many opportunities to witness double-mindedness personally. A well meaning Christian came to me one day and announced that God had called them to serve in my Church and to be available for whatever I would need them for. Unfortunately, a few months later, God called them to leave and go somewhere else. Now, either God cannot make up His mind, or the person does not really know what God wants of them.

Ironically, nothing in the Church had changed in the few months that had transpired. There weren't any fights or serious problems that had occurred. The person simply was double-minded and uncommitted.

As minister's, our aim is to bring all of our listeners into a realistic fervent relationship with God. This begins with developing theological understanding and fervency within our own hearts and willingly expressing it publically. A great Bible teaching does not end with people asking the question, "What then shall I do?" has in effect only delivered facts. God's great aim is to bring His son's and daughter's to maturity. Paul wrote, *"Him we preach, warning every man and teaching every man in all wisdom, that we may present every man perfect in Christ Jesus."* (Colossians 1:28, NKJV) "He was not satisfied to see souls saved and then to pass on. He wanted to **"present every man perfect in Christ Jesus."** (MACDONALD 1990)

Preach the Word; Live the Word

2 Timothy 4:1-2 (NLT) [1] *I solemnly urge you in the presence of God and Christ Jesus, who will someday judge the living and the dead when he appears to set up his Kingdom:* [2] *Preach the word of God. Be prepared, whether the time is favorable or not. Patiently correct, rebuke, and encourage your people with good teaching.* (New Living Translation 1996, 2004, 2007)

Preaching is proclamation of the Word of God with authority. In some religions, only priests can preach. In most protestant denominations, anyone called to preach can make proclamation. *Whether it is behind a pulpit, on a street corner, in the open air under a tent, or at a table one on one, Christian's are called by God to proclaim the truth.*

There are different levels of preaching and teaching as well as different styles. I do not intend to talk about technique, but about character and content. Each of us must develop in character as well as depth of understanding if we are going to maintain the good fight. In one way or another, all Christians have been given a message to share. Giving testimony to God's grace and power in our lives can change people's hearts.

We must always keep in mind the life of the preacher is as important as the message he preaches. In many ways, the preacher is the message. If you do not believe what you preach strong enough to live it, no one else will. Our conduct either confirms or contradicts our message. Be careful to not become an obstacle.

With God, character is primary. Many people emphasize production, the results of ministry. The worth is measured by visible accomplishments. With God, all people will be judged primarily on their conduct and secondarily on their accomplishments.

Leadership brings not only privileges but also responsibilities. Christian leaders are called to a higher calling and as leaders, according to James, will receive a stricter judgment from God, *"My brethren, let not many of you become teachers, knowing that we shall receive a stricter judgment."* (James 3:1, NKJV) "Ministry should not be undertaken lightly. Those who teach the Word of Truth will receive heavier **judgment** if they fail to practice what they teach." (MACDONALD 1990)

An example of godly character is Joseph. The Bible says of him, "*The blessings of your father have excelled the blessings of my ancestors, Up to the utmost bound of the everlasting hills. They shall be on the head of Joseph, And on the crown of the head of him who was separate from his brothers.*" (Genesis 49:26, NKJV) There were four areas of clear separation between him and his brothers: his character, determination, and devotion to God and obedience to His will. His character was so strong he resisted temptation even when it meant jail.

There are two key elements that will help a pastor develop and maintain character: God's Word and prayer. When your life is saturated with them, the blessing of God will flow out of your innermost being and ministry will be a natural result.

The Motive of Preaching

Why Preach? Do you have a motive for preaching? Paul expresses his reason for preaching in 2 Cor. 5:11, "Because we understand our fearful responsibility to the Lord, we work hard to persuade others. God knows we are sincere, and I hope you know this, too." (New Living Translation 1996, 2004, 2007)

Motive to preach begins with understanding our responsibility to the Lord. God is not going to speak out of the Heavens into the earth preaching to people. He has given us the responsibility to do this on His behalf. He has chosen to collaborate with humanity in the accomplishment of His will on earth. God wills to divinely intervene in the earth through human instruments. When He decided to intervene on behalf of man and his need for salvation, intervention came in the form of a man, the God-man, Jesus Christ. Even God's intervention on behalf of the Israelites in Egypt came through Moses.

All people are heading for judgment; their only hope of acquittal is in

Jesus Christ. How shall they then hear if no one preaches to them? Romans 10:14 (NKJV) 14 How then shall they call on Him in whom they have not believed? And how shall they believe in Him of whom they have not heard? And how shall they hear without a preacher? (The New King James Version 1982) "God sends out His servants. They preach the good news of salvation. Sinners hear God's offer of life in Christ. Some of those who hear believe the message. Those who believe call on the Lord. Those who call on Him are saved.'

"Hodge points out this is an argument founded on the principle if God wills the end, He also wills the means to reach that end. This, as we have said, is the basis of the Christian missionary movement. Paul is here vindicating his preaching the gospel to the Gentiles, a policy that the unbelieving Jews considered inexcusable. (MACDONALD 1990). The question is, If not you, then who?

Preach Powerful, Bold Sermons

Acts 19:8 (NKJV) 8 And he went into the synagogue and spoke boldly for three months, reasoning and persuading concerning the things of the kingdom of God. (The New King James Version 1982). Paul not only laid out his Gospel beliefs, he passionately persuaded his listeners of the validity and need to respond.

The Word of God itself is the final authority on doctrine and lifestyle. It is more powerful than a sharp, two-edged sword. Hebrews 4:12 (NKJV) "For the word of God is living and powerful, and sharper than any two-edged sword, piercing even to the division of soul and spirit, and of joints and marrow, and is a discerner of the thoughts and intents of the heart." (The New King James Version 1982) Since the Word is as powerful as Hebrews declares, why does it seem to not penetrate the hearts of everyone who hears it? There is a resistance to the Word in the unregenerate heart of mankind as well as intentional hindrance from the devil. (2 Corinthians 4:3-4) But even if our gospel is veiled, it is veiled to those who are perishing, whose minds the god of this age has blinded, who do not believe, lest the light of the gospel of the glory of Christ, who is the image of God, should shine on them. (The New King James Version 1982)

In the parable of the sower, the heart is represented by the soil. The first soil in the parable is called the wayward soil. It becomes hardened as people travel across it every day and trample down all signs of life. Eventually, this soil becomes so hard, nothing can penetrate it. The birds of the air represent demonic spirits that come and take away the seed sown on the hard soil. The Word cannot even have a chance to take root.

The only cure for such a hard heart is to be broken up. *"Sow for yourselves righteousness; Reap in mercy; Break up your fallow ground, For it is time to seek the LORD, Till He comes and rains righteousness on you."* (Hosea 10:12, NKJV) Before seed can be sowed or harvest reaped, the ground must be prepared and the weeds of unrighteousness must be removed.

We remain on earth as sowers to scatter good seed; as ploughmen to break up the fallow ground; as heralds publishing salvation. We are here as the "salt of the earth," to be a blessing to the world. When God's Word is sown in our hearts, it produces righteousness—changed lives and deeper commitment. This is how we as Christians are to seek the Lord.

Another reason for the seeming lack of power, I believe, is a lack of power in the preacher! When you read Acts, you find the early preachers making bold, powerful proclamations! They became a threat to the status quo. They chose to stand up and out for Jesus without care of the consequences. Any person willing to preach the truth of God's Word in the same manner will be empowered by the Spirit of God. That was the initial purpose of the Holy Spirits visitation on the Day of Pentecost (Acts 1:8) "But you shall receive power when the Holy Spirit has come upon you; and you shall be witnesses to Me in Jerusalem, and in all Judea and

Samaria, and to the end of the earth."

The factors needed to preach boldly as the Apostles did in Acts are the Holy Spirit, The Word, and a convicted, convinced, Spirit filled preacher!

If you are a professional preacher, this has probably offended you. Please realize their local professional leaders did not train many of the first preachers of the Gospel. They were considered unlearned, ignorant people. Yet, they turned the world upside down for Jesus.

I firmly believe in training, that is why I have started a Leadership Institute. However, if my training makes people dependent upon their abilities and not the Holy Spirit, I have failed them and hindered the advancement of the Kingdom of God.

Strong Preaching Attracts Sinners

Jesus' sermons attracted sinners. Luke 15:1-2 [1] Then all the tax collectors and the sinners drew near to Him to hear Him. [2] And the Pharisees and scribes complained, saying, "This Man receives sinners and eats with them." (The New King James Version 1982)

Why would bold preaching attract sinners and anger religious people? The sinners are aware they are unrighteous and unworthy. They know they need a Savior, and when they can hear the heart of Jesus in the message, they are attracted to Him. He will receive them, love them and change them without condemnation. Lost sinners came to Jesus, not because He catered to them or compromised His message, but because He cared for them. He understood their needs and tried to help them.

Religious people who are self-righteous become self-defensive are always trying to defend their personal views and are afraid to associate with sinners, defile themselves because they do not want to anger God.

Usually sermons preached by self-righteous people condemn sinners and push them away.

Before you say, "You have to compromise to get sinners to like you and listen to you," consider they loved Jesus, followed Him and changed their life. When the Gospel message is preached, people find hope and love through Jesus. Isn't that what our goal is for preaching the Gospel?

Preaching Has an Impact

(Romans 10:17) "So then faith comes by hearing, and hearing by the word of God." (The New King James Version 1982) Faith does not come through experience or age. Faith is received by the Word and is built by the Word. If you want to have an impact on the World, then preach the Word faithfully wherever you go. Strong Churches are the result of strong, Biblical preaching.

Our responsibility is to make the message as clear as possible. Colossians 4:4 (NLT) "Pray that I will proclaim this message as clearly as I should." (New Living Translation 1996, 2004, 2007) There is probably no skill that touches more areas of leadership more critically than the skill of *communicating.* Moreover, there is probably no skill in which the total person and his or her behavior are more involved in the feat. Communication is truly the swapping of meanings from person to person. The body, the apparel, the grooming, the facial expressions, the total appearance, the gestures, the symbols, the words—written or spoken or otherwise communicated—everything about a person has some part in the communicating area. No pastor-teacher can reach their optimum and not be a successful communicator.

Communication is more than just our ability to talk, but also to listen. James aptly said it this way, *"Understand this, my dear brothers and sisters: You must all be quick to listen, slow to speak, and slow to get angry. Human anger does not produce the righteousness God desires."* (James 1:19–20) (New Living Translation 1996, 2004, 2007) When people realize you are listening to them with interest, they are more likely to be engaged with you when you are speaking to them.

One time a preacher said to a group of people he had addressed that when he entered the pulpit he had no idea what he was going to preach. The people responded, "Don't worry preacher, when you finished we had no idea either!"

Do not allow unpreparedness from a lack of discipline cause you to make the message difficult to understand. If you do not understand a topic, stay away from it until you do. Not being aware of the material to be presented can become awkward and display a lack of knowledge. If the pastor is not prepared for his sermon, he will not give the congregation what they need and it will encourage them to not prepare with their whole hearts as well.

The purpose of preaching is to bring people to a realization of who God is, what He likes and what He wants. Teaching-learning effectiveness depends upon preparation for both teacher and student. In the same way, our teachers have responsibility to prepare to teach, hearers have the responsibility to prepare to learn. People need to be in awe of God, not our knowledge and great preaching abilities.

The pulpit is not a place to practice. It is a place to dispense truth, mercy and grace. We do not need any more casualties in the congregation.

Preaching and Counseling

Are these two activities separate from one another, or are they intertwined? For some, this is a dilemma creating psychological stress and an unwelcome choice to be made. The truth is they are two activities that cannot be separated but must be balanced and developed into a harmonious duo. "When Paul distinguished the preacher's two primary activities as nouthetically confronting every man and teaching every man, he had no intention of dividing these tasks" (Adams 1974, 1975, 279)

"Him we preach, warning every man and teaching every man in all wisdom, that we may present every man perfect in Christ Jesus" (Colossians 1:28, NKJV). "Here we have further insight into the ministry of the beloved apostle. It was a man-to-man ministry. He warned the unsaved of the awful wrath to come, and he taught the saints the great truths of the Christian faith. Then we see the emphasis that he placed on follow-up work. He felt a real sense of responsibility toward those whom he had pointed to the Savior. He was not satisfied to see souls saved and then to pass on." (MACDONALD 1990)

When harmonizing both preaching and counseling, we must realize that, "Each task, in turn, has as its common end the glory of God through the sanctification of God's sheep" (Adams 1974, 1975, 279).

However, many pastors feel they are not adequate for the task, the Biblical mandate calls for the pastor to be a counselor as well. Viewing Psalm 23 as a template for pastoral ministry, verse 3 says, "He restores my soul; He leads me in the paths of righteousness For His name's sake." As under shepherds of Jesus, pastors must be engaged in the task of restoration.

In the past, many pastors abandoned their posts as counselors giving rise to secular counseling practices. With it came a flood of humanistic thought based on the theory of evolution. The Bible, the very thing that could actually restore mans soul, was put aside, and the consequences have been dire. Fortunately, God, in His divine providence, has been developing a new generation of pastors that are actively restoring nouthetical counseling to its proper place.

With the new awareness of the pastoral responsibility to counsel have also come colleges and seminaries preparing the pastor for this necessary task. Volumes have now been published on the subject and are readily available to the pastor. There are virtually no excuses available for a pastor to remain ignorant and incapable of conducting his pastoral responsibility.

Once the pastor engages in the ministry of counseling, he must take the task seriously and be organized in his conduct thereof. He should not only make a commitment to the counselee, he should also expect the same from them.

The goals of the counseling should be made clear in the beginning, with a definite end in mind. No counseling should be endless. The aim of counseling is to lead the counselee to a decision to change then proceed helping them to implement these changes.

So then, the logical, Biblical conclusion we come to is that the Pastor must combine preaching and counseling to bring about the desired result: "the Glory of God in all things."

Fervency through Praise and Worship

Have you ever been in a service where a beautiful song is sung or a powerful Scripture passage read without any enthusiasm? Not very inspiring or motivating is it? Vibrant music and reading can be a tool in lifting up your spirit and stirring up passion for God.

Of course, as with all aspects of ministry, the pastor must strike a desirable balance between these two essential ministries. The pulpit is the most effective public medium for proclamation, confrontation, and the changing of lives.

When we speak of praise and worship, we immediately think of styles of music. This is a limited view of its intended meaning. Music is only one of a several ways to express praise and worship.

Praise is an expression of admiration for somebody's achievements or his or her good qualities. When you begin to verbalize all the wonderful things God has done, you are giving him praise. Of course, when you put it to music, it becomes a powerful tool in the defeating of the demonic forces and principalities in the air.

True praise begins with an attitude of gratefulness and wonder. Who can match the things God has done and will do? The answer is no one. Praise, like fervent preaching, is contagious.

True praise is also the opposite of self-centeredness. Sin brought the focus of man onto self and the subsequent result was depression, discouragement and self-defeat. The Bible says in Isaiah 61:3 "To console those who mourn in Zion, to give them beauty for ashes, the oil of joy for mourning, the garment of praise for the spirit of heaviness; that they may be called trees of righteousness, the planting of the LORD, that He may be glorified." (The New King James Version 1982) God will make a great exchange for anyone that chooses to praise Him despite his or her present circumstances.

Worship is similar to praise, yet there are differences that are significant. To worship means to love, admire, respect somebody greatly and excessively. A result of heartfelt worship is devotion and fervency. For the Christian, worship is not optional but is a part of the new nature. (John 4:24) God is Spirit, and those who worship Him must worship in spirit and truth." (The New King James Version 1982) "There must be no idea in going through a series of rituals, God is thereby pleased. Even if God instituted those rituals Himself, He still insists man approach Him with a broken and a contrite heart." (MACDONALD 1990)

The fundamental reason worship of God must be spiritual is that God is a spiritual being. People cannot worship God in any manner that may seem attractive to them. They must worship Him as He by the Spirit has revealed we should. The prerequisite is to be born again (John 3:3) Jesus answered and said to him, "Most assuredly, I say to you, unless one is born again, he cannot see the kingdom of God." (The New King James

Version 1982)

Worship, expressed through music, is a love song to God. It lifts us to a higher level of intimacy with God because we are putting Him in a higher place in our lives. Only a true believer in Christ is able to enter this level of intimacy with God. All others will stand by not understanding why you are expressing yourself in that manner. They do not have a clue as to what is going on.

I want to take a moment to express how important musically carried praise and worship is when it comes to engaging in spiritual warfare. The Bible says, *"For the weapons of our warfare are not carnal but mighty in God for pulling down strongholds, casting down arguments and every high thing that exalts itself against the knowledge of God, bringing every thought into captivity to the obedience of Christ,"* (2 Corinthians 10:4–5, NKJV) We are given spiritual weapons that are powerful. These weapons are the Word of God, the Name of Jesus and the Blood of Jesus. Music becomes the instrument that releases the spiritual weaponry directly at the enemy. When you engage believers corporately into the act of praise and worship, you release a stronger onslaught against the enemy.

Consistent practice of fervent, Christ-centered, music will result in the Heavens being opened and the power of God being released in our midst. *(Psalm 68:2) As smoke is driven away, so drive them away; as wax melts before the fire, so let the wicked perish at the presence of God.* (The New King James Version 1982)

Christians teach and admonish one another when they worship together. New believers learn how to live as the children of God when they watch the older saints worshiping in spirit and in truth.

Fervency through Prayer

James 5:16 (NKJV) Confess your trespasses to one another, and pray for one another, that you may be healed. The effective, fervent prayer of a righteous man avails much. (The New King James Version 1982)

Prayer is a discipline that brings us into contact with God and His power. The prayer of an individual whose heart is right with God accomplishes much. God has chosen to act in conjunction with the faith and requests of His followers. Though He could do anything at any time, His choice is to work in and through the Church.

In the text quoted above, the phrase, "the effectual fervent" is actually one word in the Greek text. The word is "energeo" which means to put forth power. Our English equivalent is energy. This is not referring to quiet, gentle prayer. The picture here is of a person who is passionately seeking God.

For the early disciples, there was a time designated for prayer (Acts 3:1). By establishing a particular time in the day for prayer, it develops into a part of our lifestyle. To miss that time leaves us feeling as if we missed an important part of our lives. It is more than a duty; it is a time of developing a relationship with God through communion with Him.

Prayer should be as natural to a Christian as eating and drinking. In the beginning of establishing a prayer life, it comes hard with resistance coming from not only the flesh but the devil as well. Desire is essential to beginning. After time, your desire will give way to delight.

You must determine the best time for you to set aside for prayer. What can you give up or rearrange so you can have quality time in prayer? With the many distractions available to us today, we need to carefully guard this time of intimate contact with God.

The key element to effective prayer is the Holy Spirit Himself. There are several Scriptures related to this: Jude 20 (NKJV) [20] But you, beloved, building yourselves up on your most holy faith, praying in the Holy Spirit,

Ephesians 6:18 (NKJV) [18] praying always with all prayer and supplication in the Spirit, being watchful to this end with all perseverance and supplication for all the saints—

Romans 8:26-27 (NKJV) [26] Likewise the Spirit also helps in our weaknesses. For we do not know what we should pray for as we ought, but the Spirit Himself makes intercession for us with groanings which cannot be uttered. [27] Now He who searches the hearts knows what the mind of the Spirit *is,* because He makes intercession for the saints according to *the will of* God.

Galatians 4:6 (NKJV) [6] and because you are sons, God has sent forth the Spirit of His Son into your hearts, crying out, "Abba, Father!" (The New King James Version 1982)

The greatest prayer partner in the world is the Holy Spirit Himself. He knows the heart of God as well as the Perfect Will of God. Trust Him when you are praying. Listen to His voice and promptings and you will find your prayers are being answered.

We have to be willing to let go of our control and surrender our will to God in prayer. Remember, "Father knows best." Submission to God as the Sovereign is difficult for anyone that tries to maintain control, for it requires us to accept God's plan even when it does not seem clear.

Finally, when developing your prayer life, grow into it gradually. You may not be able to pray for hours on end yet, but there will come a time when it can happen. As a personal prayer life is developed, it will be shaped more and more by an awareness of the presence of God.

Strong prayer will develop strong spirits. Strong spirits will enable Christians to endure in the time of battle for themselves as well as others.

I want to have strong, fervent Christians praying for me when I have a serious situation.

Please understand there is a time when we need to be quiet in the presence of God. The other side to praying is listening! We cannot hear God if we are doing all of the talking. While methods and practices may vary according to personality, the common factor of listening prayer should be an open Bible and reading, meditating on what is there and allowing the Holy Spirit to show how to apply it. Open your spiritual ears and you will hear God speak to.

There is no obstacle between earth and heaven. God hears our praises and prayers. We can ask him for anything within His revealed will. We can live without hypocrisy and like Elijah in the old days; our faithful prayer can change the world.

Chapter Five

The Second Purpose of the Church

In this chapter, we will examine the second purpose derived from Matt. 22:37-40, To Be a Functional Family of God. There are two definitions to functional that apply; serving a useful purpose and in good working order.

To Be a Functional Family of God

Let us examine the opposite characteristic first; dysfunction. A definition of dysfunction is a disturbance in the usual pattern of activity or behavior.

It does not take long and you do not have to look hard before you can see dysfunction in any gathering of people. Every Church has to deal with the reality that most of the people that become a part of their fellowship are dysfunctional. In a fallen world, dysfunction actually is normal. Our mission in this aspect is to move people from dysfunction into functioning fully for God. Of course, the question is, "how?"

There are three basic functions that will bring the Church to a place it is functioning at its utmost potential; Fellowship, Edification and Release into individual ministry gifts. Though there may be many others, others will grow from these keys.

Fellowship

Acts 2:42 (NKJV) "and they continued steadfastly in the apostles' doctrine and fellowship, in the breaking of bread, and in prayers." (The New King

James Version 1982) From its inception on the Day of Pentecost, the early Church became a thriving, growing organism bringing great glory to the Lord Jesus Christ. This passage reveals the basic functions they were developing. The key function that was bringing about cohesiveness was fellowship.

As we discussed in the previous chapter, Fellowship is a sharing of common interests, goals, experiences or views. Christian fellowship centers on Jesus Christ and His purposes for us as His followers.

For many, fellowship means getting together, eating food and just talking. Though that may be an aspect of fellowship, it can be very shallow and keep us from accomplishing our mission. The amount of time spent is not as important as the quality and focus. When true comradery exists, the plans and purposes of God will be fulfilled.

The first step to experiencing true fellowship is learning about each other's history. The more you learn about someone's personal history, the more you will understand him or her. This requires time and patience, which is an invaluable investment that will yield great dividends in the end. This is equally applicable in developing fervency with God. He has revealed Himself to us in the Scriptures and we have the responsibility to seek Him to know Him.

History sharing in an effort to develop interpersonal relationships requires vulnerability. When you begin to share about your past, you are at risk of experiencing rejection, ridicule and even misunderstanding. However, the benefits far outweigh the risks.

In Luke 15:4-7, Jesus taught in a parable the importance of rescuing the lost sheep. In order to save the lost sheep, the shepherd had to leave the 99. The risk of leaving the 99 was outweighed by the importance of the one. The risk was not an uncalculated one that would cause great harm; it was calculated, weighed out and executed. That is the kind of risk we need to be willing to take in establishing and developing relationships.

The second step to follow is affirmation. Simply put what we are saying is,

"I know who you are and I'm getting to know your strengths and weaknesses, and I love you anyway." Affirmation must be with more than words; it must be demonstrated with actions that follow the verbal assertion. When a person is feeling down and they are at their low point, having friends that are committed to them and their purposes in God can be reassuring and comforting.

You may learn a person's history but if you are unwilling to accept them for who they are and commit to their welfare, your relationship will not go any further. God the Father knows our history better than we do and He has expressed and demonstrated His commitment to us and our well being. A Biblical example is *"For I know the thoughts that I think toward you, says the LORD, thoughts of peace and not of evil, to give you a future and a hope."* Jeremiah 29:11 (The New King James Version 1982)

One of the purposes of building relationships is to further the cause of Christ together. Teamwork is more effective than individual stars performing on their own. There is an exponential increase in ability and effectiveness through teamwork.

Another purpose in relationships is personal development. We need people in our lives that love us for who we are but are willing to be honest with us so we can overcome our weaknesses. In order to be effective requires positive affirmation of each other and realistic self-evaluation.

As a rule of thumb, if you are involved in someone's life and need to confront an issue, begin with positive affirmation, deal with the issue and finish with positive affirmation. It might hurt, but affirmation will lessen the pain and go a long way to conquering the fear of rejection. Moreover, once an issue has been addressed, it needs to stay private. Relationships have been destroyed and ministry effectiveness diminished by talebearers.

Now, you can enter the arena of fellowship. Getting to this point is a process that requires work and commitment, but again, it pays dividends. At this point sharing can begin and true friendship experienced.

I want to close this section by adding we have a responsibility to affirm each other in regards to God's relationship with us. Reminding each other of how much God loves us and wants us to succeed is beneficial. Paul instructed the Corinthian's to make sure the use of the gifts brought edification *"Even so you, since you are zealous for spiritual gifts, let it be for the edification of the church that you seek to excel."* 1 Corinthians 14:12 (The New King James Version 1982)

Edification

True Biblical fellowship will produce an environment where edification can exist. *Romans 14:19 Therefore let us pursue the things which make for peace and the things by which one may edify another.* (The New King James Version 1982)

2 Corinthians 12:19 (NKJV) [19] Again, do you think we excuse ourselves to you? We speak before God in Christ. But we do all things, beloved, for your edification. (The New King James Version 1982) Paul expresses here he was more interested in edifying the Corinthian's than protecting his own reputation.

In the context of relationships, edification is a building up morally and spiritually by building one another's faith. Mutual edification means we are looking out for each other. Edification occurs through encouragement and teaching.

Our objective as individuals is to not cause other people to stumble and to reject judgmental attitudes. Both action and attitude can affect the welfare of other people. The extremes to avoid are being too lenient or being too strict. A fair balance can be achieved. In this balance is where people can be given the space and time to grow. Rather than tear down. Practice building up.

Edification is premised on the command to love our neighbor as ourselves. The greatest need apart from salvation we as humans have is to be loved. We crave love from our parents when we are infants and as we grow, we look for love from others. Rejection is the hardest experience to overcome because it says we were not worthy of love. Finding someone to love us takes time and patience.

The best way to find love is to give love. The Bible does teach whatever we sow we will reap if we do not give up (Gal 6). Nature teaches us we reap in kind. In other words, you will get back whatever seed you put into the ground.

How much do your activities center on your care and comfort? This is how you love yourself. It is not an emotional love, but a real, genuine love that provides. The same care and concern we exercise for ourselves is the same we should show toward others.

Remember, only those who have been born again can love in this manner. It takes the supernatural power of the Holy Spirit to love like this through us. Any other kind of love is from the flesh and usually has a hidden motive behind it.

Loving our neighbor in this manner is also unconditional. We do not love if we are loved; we love even if we are hated. Loving your enemy goes a long way!

Matthew 5:43-48 (NKJV) [43] "You have heard it was said, 'You shall love your neighbor and hate your enemy.' [44] But I say to you, love your enemies, bless those who curse you, do good to those who hate you, and pray for those who spitefully use you and persecute you, [45] that you may be sons of your Father in heaven; for He makes His sun rise on the evil and on the good, and sends rain on the just and on the unjust. [46] For if you love those who love you, what rewards have you? Do not even the tax collectors do the same? [47] And if you greet your brethren only, what do you do more than others? Do not even the tax collectors do so? [48] Therefore you shall be perfect, just as your Father in heaven is perfect. (The New King James Version 1982)

You do not have to be Christian for very long before you have an opportunity to practice what Jesus said here. If you do not have any enemies, maybe you are hiding under a rock!

As a servant of God, you are His ambassador, calling people unto repentance toward God. God's heart is to reach the sinner and save his soul. He cannot do it if we are fighting with them. Unsaved people practice sin because that is what they are programmed to do. They are living under the curse of Adam's nature, just as we did. Someone loved you when you were not very lovable. Return the favor.

Christians make mistakes; be forgiving and love them anyway. Christians do foolish things; love them anyway. Be longsuffering toward people and you will be used by God to bring back the backslider to repentance before God.

A Test of Love

1 John 2:9-11 (NKJV) [9] He who says he is in the light, and hates his brother, is in darkness until now. [10] He who loves his brother abides in the light, and there is no cause for stumbling in him. [11] But he who hates his brother is in darkness and walks in darkness, and does not know where he is going, because the darkness has blinded his eyes. (The New King James Version 1982)

A believer who hates his brother has lost his spiritual perspective and sense of direction. *Where there is an absence of love, there is the presence of hate. There is not a middle ground here. Hate will eat away at your spirit until bitterness, wrath and anger spew out of your mouth. It is a dangerous thing to allow hurts and disappointments to turn into hatred.*

Leaders cannot allow persecution and opposition to create hatred in their heart. As Jesus forgave, so must we. Walking in an attitude of forgiveness will enable us to continue to love as Christ has loved us.

The Ability to Love

Romans 5:5 (NKJV) "Now hope does not disappoint, because the love of God has been poured out in our hearts by the Holy Spirit who was given to us." (The New King James Version 1982)

God has given us the ability to love even our enemies by pouring out His love into our hearts. When we are born-again, the Holy Spirit brings everything we need including the love of God. We cannot love in our own power; we have to love in and through the power of God. 2 Peter 1:3 (NKJV) [3] as His divine power has given to us all things that pertain to life and godliness, through the knowledge of Him who called us by glory and virtue. (The New King James Version 1982)

To believe that we cannot love nor do anything else God requires is to directly contradict the Scriptures. There will be times you feel incapable. When this happens, remind yourself God has given you everything you need to be godly and live life to the fullest.

Finally, you must understand love does not mean you will like everything that others do. It does not mean you have to tolerate bad behavior or give in to the selfishness of people who want to use you. Love can and must be able to say no. A true manifestation of love will do what is best for others, not necessarily what they want.

People will try to take advantage of your kindness. Know where to draw the line in love! Love God first and foremost, and He will guide you in all things. Jesus loved but He was not controlled by the whims and fanciful ideas of people, especially the religious leaders of His day.

As a leader, be aware of any attitudes that may cause you to manifest anything other than the love of God.

Chapter Six

To Be Fishers of Men

These last two purposes we are about to examine deal with the functional aspect of the four-fold purposes of the Church as well as the mission of the Church. As I stated earlier, to be balanced we need all four purposes operating in our lives and our Churches. *Matthew 28:17-28 (NKJV) [17] When they saw Him, they worshiped Him; but some doubted. [18] And Jesus came and spoke to them, saying, "All authority has been given to Me in heaven and on earth. [19] Go therefore and make disciples of all the nations, baptizing them in the name of the Father and of the Son and of the Holy Spirit, [20] teaching them to observe all things that I have commanded you; and lo, I am with you always, even to the end of the age." Amen.* (The New King James Version 1982)

"Go therefore and make..." this is a command, an imperative, not a suggestion. This is not to be taken lightly by any means. Evangelism is a Church function and not just a few individuals. There are many ways to evangelize your community, state, country and the world. Personality and culture play a large part in the styles of evangelism. Cultural awareness becomes essential in determining the manner evangelism will be conducted.

Understand, the methods of evangelism will vary from Church to Church, but the message of the Gospel must stay the same. For example, if you live in an area frequently evangelized by a cult, you must carefully consider their methods and seek to do something that does not replicate them. People will be conditioned to reject what they have been approached with. Take the time to study the behaviors and cultural practices of the area you are seeking to evangelize. Cultural relevance will open doors that no man can close. Stay true to the Biblical revelation of the Gospel and the Lord will reward your efforts.

Jesus said to go and make disciples. Notice he did not tell us to go and make converts to our particular belief systems. They are His disciples and we are His servants. If you continue to practice this, you will do well.

Evangelism, the Door to the Church

Many people may attend Church services on any given day and even perform tasks, but not everyone attending or participating are actually a part of the Church. The true Church of Jesus Christ is made up of people who have entered through the reception of the Gospel message, which is delivered through evangelism.

The goal of the Church in the area of evangelism is to get the people through the doors. I refer to this as Front Door Evangelism. One of the keys to this is relevance. How many times have you seen a program that was not relevant to the people in the community bring success? Rarely if ever will an irrelevant program produce results.

For too long, the Church has ignored topics of interest and problems that communities are facing. Jesus showed concern for the people He met. He was moved with compassion and as a result, performed miracles on their behalf. His greatest contention was with the religious leaders who constantly fought Him. Their greatest fear was they would lose their place of prominence in Israel. As a result, they were ineffective in helping the people of Israel.

Perhaps the ineffectiveness of our age is a result of being afraid to lose a place of prominence in the religious world. Instead of helping the down and out, we rail on them to the applause of the religious community. The result is alienation from the very people that need salvation through Jesus Christ.

I believe the Church needs to return to loving the less desirable and the ostracized of the community. Can you imagine what will happen if we actually start caring for those around us? Perhaps they would be lining up at our doors, anxious to hear what we have to say because we have spoken so loudly and clearly through community intervention.

Once you can get the community through the doors of the Church, you create an opportunity to present the Gospel powerfully and clearly.

A Bigger Picture of Evangelism

In order to fulfill the command, we need to move outside of our communities and into the world. While this may be difficult for some to physically participate in, they can nevertheless help through prayer and financial support.

As we develop new disciples, we must also train them to share their faith with others. Some will even be called to go out from the local Church and take the Gospel to every creature on the earth.

As disciples move through the process of maturation, they will also develop needful and helpful relationships such as we discussed in previous chapters. Through this, God will open doors of opportunity for them that no other person would be able to understand or fulfill.

Jesus' plan for evangelism was one of simplicity but was nonetheless profound. His effectiveness was related to focusing on a few men to equip them and turn them loose upon their world. He did not use a classroom setting for His training; He used on the job training. They witnessed Him as He ministered to individuals as well as crowds.

Jesus' method was to teach the disciples as they went about daily routines. Many of His teachings recorded in the New Testament were directed toward the disciples while others listened in. He taught them how to face adversity, persecution and even natural disasters. His favorite form of teaching was parables and He often explained them to the disciples but not to the crowds.

Jesus' plan of evangelism may not appeal to the modern Church builder, but the results are indisputable. He was more concerned with the long-term results than short-term flashes of success. This could explain the short shelf life of many Churches. They disappear almost as quickly as they come.

The selection of the twelve was not according to social class, financial position or educational achievements. Prayer preceded the selection of the twelve and each picked according to the will of God. The good news for modern man as he studies the life of the disciples is that God can take any willing person and transform them into leaders that can shake the world.

The account of Gideon shows the ability of God to do great things with small groups in the beginning. One of the key lessons learned from this account of Gideon is God can work effectively through small groups to affect the whole.

When Moses had an encounter with God in the wilderness, God asked him what he had in his hand. All Moses had at the time was his shepherd's staff. God had him cast it on the ground and it became a snake. Then, to Moses' dismay, God actually told him to pick up the snake. When he did, it turned back into a staff (see Exodus 4). There was nothing magical about his staff. It was just an ordinary stick! The point God was making with Moses was that God could do anything with anybody, no matter what they have or do not have.

Trust God with what you do have and He will perform great miracles with you and through you. If you have a small ministry, present it to God and ask Him to use it and multiply your efforts. Do not allow a crooked stick to keep you from God's best. Little is much when God is in it.

Do not view the world as an impossible task for your Church. Join people of like vision and conquer the world for Jesus.

Chapter Seven

Facilitating Fully Devoted Followers

Matthew 28:17-20 (NKJV) [17] When they saw Him, they worshiped Him; but some doubted. [18] And Jesus came and spoke to them, saying, "All authority has been given to Me in heaven and on earth. [19] Go therefore and make disciples of all the nations, baptizing them in the name of the Father and of the Son and of the Holy Spirit, [20] teaching them to observe all things that I have commanded you; and lo, I am with you always, even to the end of the age." Amen. (The New King James Version 1982)

The fourth purpose, like the third, comes from the Great Commission. Jesus said "teach them to observe whatsoever I have commanded you." What was one of the commands? Go and make disciples of all nations.

The three stages necessary for a Christian are Win, Train, and Release. The purpose of winning new souls is to train them to do the same. We create a cycle that is essential to the perpetuating of the Christian faith.

A Spirit filled, Spirit led Christian who desires to become an agent of impartation must of necessity move toward a life of demonstration. The Master demonstrated to His disciples everything they would need to know to achieve success after His departure. It was through such demonstration His disciples grew hungry for what Jesus had. He never forced any of them into practicing and spiritual disciplines; He always created a hunger by being a model.

With great confidence, Paul encouraged the believers in Corinth to follow his example. *"And you should imitate me, just as I imitate Christ."* (1 Corinthians 11:1, NLT) *"He renounced personal advantages and rights in order to help those about him. The Corinthians should do likewise, and not selfishly parade their freedoms in such a way as to hinder the gospel of Christ or offend the weak brother."* (MACDONALD 1990)

"Dear brothers and sisters, pattern your lives after mine, and learn from those who follow our example." (Philippians 3:17, NLT) Believers are the living example of the truth of the Scriptures. *Lehman Strauss comments:*

Paul considered himself the recipient of God's mercy that he might be a "pattern"; thus his whole life, subsequent to his conversion, was dedicated to presenting to others an outline sketch of what a Christian should be. "God saved Paul in order that he might show by the example of his conversion what Jesus Christ did for him He can and will do for others. Was not this the special object our Lord had in view in extending His mercy to you and me? I believe He has saved us to be a pattern to all future believers. Are we serving as examples of those who have been saved by His grace? May it be so?" (MACDONALD 1990)

Leaders must live transparent lives before those they are equipping, both the good and the bad. Through the bad times, they should see their leaders apologizing when necessary, in the good times, reflecting the praise to God who alone is worthy.

I believe one of the hardest parts of ministry we face is releasing people into meaningful ministries, especially if it means that they may go out from us into another part of the harvest. Gifted people are hard to come by and the thought of losing them causes dread. However, in God's Kingdom, when we give, we get back in larger proportions. Winning, training and releasing are the keys to increase in your congregation.

Not everyone we train is going to leave us. Many are called to serve in the local Church and are quite content to do that. They need to be effectively trained and given opportunity to release their gifting into the Body of

Christ.

Release into Meaningful Ministry

I want to begin this section by emphasizing there is a distinct difference between ministry and mission. A minister is one who serves others, thus ministry occurs in the context of the church and is developed there as well. Mission's are the church's focus outside of the fellowship towards the lost with the objective of winning them to Christ.

The question is often asked of trainers as to why all these other things must occur before releasing people into ministry. Why not skip relationship building and just move into ministry? The answer to that is, "the essence of ministry is relationship." Christianity is not a religion that practices rites with no substance. The very nature of Christianity is relationship. First, we have a relationship with God through Jesus Christ; secondly, we have a relationship with one another also through Jesus Christ.

A viable definition of Ministry is the impartation of life; True life is found in Jesus Christ. Jesus said, "I am the Way, the Truth and the Life; no man comes to the Father but by Me. (John 14:6)" (The New King James Version 1982). Therefore, true ministry focuses on bringing people into a living relationship with God through Jesus Christ. In essence, as a minister, you cannot give what you do not have.

When Jesus sent the Holy Spirit on the Day of Pentecost, He was imparting to the faithful disciples His very own Spirit. The enablement for ministry came through the empowering of the Spirit, not a classroom or college diploma. Learning was infused with the very power of God and it was effective in accomplishing the agenda of Jesus Christ in the earth.

All truly Biblical ministries become avenues for the impartation of life. As believers allow the internal working of the Holy Spirit to flow through them into the lives of others, they become agents of the dispensing of God's grace.

Paul taught the Ephesians to be continually filled with the Spirit. *"Don't be drunk with wine, because that will ruin your life. Instead, be filled with the Holy Spirit,"* (Ephesians 5:18, NLT) Just as a person who is drunk with wine is under the power of alcohol, so a Spirit-filled believer is controlled and empowered by the Spirit.

As relationships are discovered and developed, meaningful ministry can occur. When we allow others to have access to us, mutual edification will result in mutual gift discovery. You may be able to see someone else's gift they are having a hard time discovering. In an environment of trust, this can be shared and developed.

Timing is essential in releasing into meaningful ministry. Begin with small steps and develop from there. Not everyone is ready to travel and conduct crusades, but they may be ready to go on a crusade of one! Ministry develops over time and through careful exercise of the gifts.

Proper training precedes delegation and delegation is followed up with inspection and encouragement. There is an old saying that is appropriate here, "Inspect what you expect." (Source unknown) Jesus usually spent time in reflection with the disciples after He had sent them on a mission. This gave them an opportunity to share with Him and their fellow disciples, thus bolstering the faith of all the disciples.

Jesus also used the failures and setbacks of His disciples as an opportunity to instruct them further. When they questioned why they could not cast a demon out of a young boy, Jesus took the opportunity to teach on prayer and fasting (Mark 9:17-29). They were able to comprehend His teaching because Jesus also demonstrated them as well. In effective delegating, there must be allowance for some difference from the rate or quality of productivity the leader might require of him.

Under His supervision, He was careful, not allowing them to rest too much after success or quit after setbacks and failures. He taught from their mistakes as well as their success and urged them to move forward.

Jesus never demanded perfection in His disciple's efforts; He did expect their best. He was a Master at building the disciples up so they could reach greater heights than they had before. Leaders cannot do any less today.

I am a firm believer there is something for every Christian to do. If people do not find something meaningful in the Church they are attending, they may either regress or leave and go where they can find purpose.

If you are doing more than one ministry in the Church, ask why? Is it because there is a lack of commitment or is it a lack of shared opportunity. Instead of doing it all, build relationships and release people to help you. A person who finds purpose and meaning in the Church is a person who is committed for the long haul. Are you stealing someone's opportunity?

Developing Potential Leaders

Where do we begin to train potential leaders? Training needs to be developed based on two major criteria, Purpose and Mission.

In this dissertation, we have identified the four major purposes of the Church and Christian individually. From purpose, through prayer and Bible reading, the mission of your ministry will emerge. As the mission for you personally and for your Church becomes clear, you use that to develop your training.

When you look at your mission, you have to ask the question, how then do I do this? The, "what and the how" determine the areas and degree of emphasis. Every ministry is different.

The geographical setting has much to do with how you carry out your mission. If you are going to be reaching out into communities nearby, you have to research the demographics. Children's outreach will not work well in a community of retired citizens! You may have a strong ministry team to youth and children, but the absence of these youth will result in an ineffective ministry. You will have to gear your training to senior adults.

It is important to match the calling and the gifting with appropriate training. One size fits all leadership training just will not be effective. There is a need for doctrinal and theological training for everyone, but then you also need to specialize with different ministries.

You will discover some people will change their direction as they pursue their individual studies. What they believe they want to do today can change as they develop a relationship with God and go deeper into His Word. Glamour and glory are very attractive to some and this is the basis of desire for many. After spending time in training and actual hands on ministry, the glamour and glory disappear, leaving us to come face to face with reality. It is at this point many realize their real calling from God.

At the Leadership Institute of New England in New Britain, Ct, our first year emphasis is on the essence of leadership. The students are introduced to the theory that all are leaders because everyone has a degree of influence over other people. When they are finished with the first year of studies, they are ready to help lead the Church in its mission.

The second year involves doctrinal and theological studies. The students are also taught the mission and ministry of the Church. This includes a thorough study of ministry as revealed in Ephesians 4 as well as Romans 12.

All Christians are called to be ministers and we all need to be trained. If you are a pastor, I encourage you to become involved in training your congregation for the work of ministry. If you are a member of a Church, commit yourself to the purposes of the Church and assist your pastor in fulfilling the Great Commission.

Character Development

As a part of training for ministry, character development must not be overlooked. Too many times character flaws are overlooked because a person is so gifted or has a strong influence over others. The Apostle Paul instructed Timothy on selecting leaders for the Church. When you read the qualifications in First Timothy 3, there are 16 listed for a person who desires to be an elder. Of them, two have to do with ability and 14 with character.

Effective life change encompasses the entire man, not just his brain. The purpose of teaching is life transformation. "Don't copy (be conformed to) the behavior and customs of this world, but let God transform you into a new person by changing the way you think. Then you will learn to know God's will for you, which is good and pleasing and perfect." Romans 12:2, (New Living Translation 1996, 2004, 2007)

Transformation is a life process that works from within and affects the outer man. Consequently, it must involve the "heart" to accomplish its goal. The heart includes the will, the mind and the emotions as well.

The Bible commands caution regarding the heart. *"Guard your heart above all else, for it determines the course of your life"* Proverbs 4:23, (New Living Translation 1996, 2004, 2007). The heart is the reservoir of all wisdom and the source of whatever affects life and character. *"A good person produces good things from the treasury of a good heart, and an evil person produces evil things from the treasury of an evil heart."* (Matthew 12:35, NLT) *"For from the heart come evil thoughts, murder, adultery, all sexual immorality, theft, lying, and slander."* (Matthew 15:19, NLT).

To be a person of impact requires winning the heart of the student gaining the right to be heard. Jesus teaches us the Student will become as their teacher *"Students are not greater than their teacher. But the student who is fully trained will become like the teacher."* (Luke 6:40) (New Living Translation 1996, 2004, 2007)

Leaders will be judged at a higher standard than followers will. *James 3:1 (NKJV)* [1]*" My brethren, let not many of you become teachers, knowing that we shall receive a stricter judgment."* (The New King James Version 1982) Leaders are judged not only by their teaching abilities, but they are also judged by their conduct. *"Live wisely among those who are not believers, and make the most of every opportunity. Let your conversation be gracious and attractive so that you will have the right response for everyone."* (Colossians 4:5–6) (New Living Translation 1996, 2004, 2007)

One only has to look at the recent history of the Church to realize that achieving great success in ministry can suddenly be washed away by misconduct. Ministers have had worldwide influence yet at the same time they had hidden character issues that eventually manifested and choked out their work. Could this be what Jesus was talking about in the parable of the sower when he referred to the cares of this life and the deceitfulness of riches rising up and choking out the Word?

Character cannot be instilled simply through classroom instruction; it is something that is caught more than taught. Therefore, true Christ-like character must be demonstrated by leader's who set the bar high and do not excuse themselves from personal responsibility. So then, the two essential ingredients to true discipleship, teaching and modeling, are realized through the mentoring relationship.

The testing ground of character is real life circumstances. *"And not only that, but we also glory in tribulations, knowing that tribulation produces perseverance; and perseverance, character; and character, hope."* (Romans 5:3–4) (The New King James Version 1982) So then, since character is developed through tribulation, which produces perseverance, and character must be demonstrated, leaders must live transparent lives for the benefit of those that follow.

Character is contagious. Behavior may be a result of choices, but those choices are formed by watching other people handle similar issues. This is why the conduct of a leader has to be brought under stricter scrutiny; they affect others by their own behavior. Jesus taught about the importance of godly influence. *""You are the salt of the earth; but if the salt loses its flavor, how shall it be seasoned? It is then good for nothing but to be thrown out and trampled underfoot by men. "You are the light of the world. A city that is set on a hill cannot be hidden. Nor do they light a lamp and put it under a basket, but on a lampstand, and it gives light to all who are in the house. Let your light so shine before men, that they may see your good works and glorify your Father in heaven "* (Matthew 5:13–16) (The New King James Version 1982). "The disciple has one great function: to be **the salt of the earth** by living out the terms of discipleship listed in the Beatitudes and throughout the rest of the Sermon. If he fails to exhibit this spiritual reality, men will tread his testimony under their feet. The world has only contempt for an undedicated believer." (MACDONALD 1990)

Character is a manifestation of maturity. Maturity is a measurement of Christ-likeness. The goal of ministry according to Paul in Eph. 4 is to arrive at the fullness and stature of Jesus. Time alone cannot produce maturity; it is developed as we willingly submit ourselves to the Holy Spirit in every situation we face and allow Him to apply the principles of Christianity to our lives.

Proverbs 20:11 (NKJV) [11] Even a child is known by his deeds whether what he does is pure and right; Matthew 7:20 (NKJV) [20] Therefore by their fruits you will know them. (The New King James Version 1982)

A person's conduct reveals his true character. The root determines the fruit. An apple tree may tell you it is a peach tree, but at harvest, time the apple will provide contrary evidence and the truth will then be evident.

Over time, the true character of a person will be revealed. There is only so long a person can cover up his true nature. This is one of the reasons why we are instructed to not put novices into leadership positions. Ultimately, they will damage those that are subjected to their incompetence in leadership.

Character matters. As you are developing personally, make sure you mature and become more like Christ. If you desire to be a leader, be patient and allow God to develop your character. When the time is right, you will be leading.

Chapter Eight

God's Agenda

God's agenda is people. He is "the Good Shepherd." In Luke 4:18, Jesus defined His ministry: *"The Spirit of the LORD is upon Me, Because He has anointed Me To preach the gospel to the poor; He has sent Me to heal the brokenhearted, To proclaim liberty to the captives And recovery of sight to the blind, To set at liberty those who are oppressed;* (The New King James Version 1982)

Love God, Love People

You cannot survive long in ministry if you do not have love. *Matthew 22:34-40 (NKJV) 34 But when the Pharisees heard that He had silenced the Sadducees, they gathered together. 35 Then one of them, a lawyer, asked Him a question, testing Him, and saying, 36 "Teacher, which is the great commandment in the law?" 37 Jesus said to him, 'You shall love the Lord your God with all your heart, with all your soul, and with all your mind.' 38 This is the first and great commandment. 39 And the second is like it: 'You shall love your neighbor as yourself.' 40 On these two commandments hang all the Law and the Prophets."* (The New King James Version 1982)

Jesus' mission was not to establish an institution that required talented people to run it. He came for the purpose of bringing hope, healing, deliverance and purpose to the people He created.

God's business is transforming people's lives into the image of Jesus Christ. Paul shared with the Roman Christians, *""For whom He foreknew, He also predestined to be conformed to the image of His Son, that He might be the firstborn among many brethren"* (Romans 8:29, NKJV) (The New King James Version 1982). Conformation through transformation is a lifelong process and God is committed to finishing that which He has begun; Philippians *1:6 "being confident of this very thing that He who has begun a good work in you will complete it until the day of Jesus Christ"* (The New King James Version 1982). God worked a wonderful transformation in the Philippians when He first saved them. Paul has no apprehension the God who has begun to work in them will leave them now. How good to know God is totally dedicated to you and to me. He will continue His transforming work until it is wonderfully completed when Jesus comes.

Since God is a people oriented God, it is a logical conclusion His Church needs to be people friendly. People, with all of their problems, are a part of the mission. God wants to intervene in the affairs of humanity, returning us to His original purposes. He meets us where we are and begins the work of transformation. The Church must return to loving the unlovable and allowing God to work through it to change people's lives.

What are you doing as a Church to nurture people back into health? Do your ministry programs reflect love for God and compassion for people who are in need? I believe the validity of programs is not determined by how many people participate, but by their purposes and objectives determined by God's Word and their cultural setting.

There are not any prerequisites to receive ministry from the Church. When Jesus ministered to people, He did not ask His disciples if those seeking Him had joined His ministry, were tithing faithfully, and had faithfully attended His meetings. He ministered to them because they were His mission. As the sower from the parable, we must be non-discriminate in ministering to those present in our services. Non-judgmental attitudes toward all who seek prayer are essential in fulfilling

God's agenda in reaching all humanity. The Apostle Paul clearly articulated, *"Therefore I exhort first of all that supplications, prayers, intercessions, and giving of thanks be made for all men, for kings and all who are in authority, that we may lead a quiet and peaceable life in all godliness and reverence. For this is good and acceptable in the sight of God our Savior, who desires all men to be saved and to come to the knowledge of the truth"* (1 Timothy 2:1–4) (The New King James Version 1982).

Do not view people as an interruption to your ministry; see them as your target! God anoints His servant's so that through them intervene in their lives. You cannot honestly create an agenda that will not be interrupted from time to time by unexpected visitors or even a crisis. As a leader, use wisdom and discernment when an interruption occurs. Do not be hasty in putting people off until a more opportune time for you. The writer of Hebrews cautions us in this matter, *""Do not forget to entertain strangers, for by so doing some have unwittingly entertained angels"* (Hebrews 13:2) (The New King James Version 1982)

Though it may seem to be contradictory, in all fairness, we have to objectively examine the motives of people seeking further ministry than the altar call. This may seem unfair, but the devil can plant people in your ministry that really don't want help from you; all they want to do is drain you by using you as a trash can to dump their anger and unbelief upon. They will walk away satisfied for the moment, but no real change will occur in their life. This is not a result of the minister's failure, but a natural result of people who want to hold onto their problems for getting attention.

Some people view the Church as a social welfare source, always taking but never giving. They actually do not want God to heal them or restore them; they want to hang on to their old, sinful lifestyles and reap the benefits of a child of God. God loves them and we should also; however, love does what is best for the person, not always what the person wants.

So how do we handle people like this? I recommend praying first for discernment and then, as in all things, pray for a revelation of God's will. An example of this can be found in Joshua chapter 9. Without taking counsel from God, the Israelites were deceived by cities they were supposed to destroy. They made a hasty covenant with them and thus missed what God had for them. Remember this, "Things are not always as they seem."

God is the Initiator

God has taken all of the initiatives to reach the lost world. Man does not seek God; God seeks man. *Psalm 14:2-3 (NKJV) ² The LORD looks down from heaven upon the children of men, To see if there are any who understand, who seek God. ³ They have all turned aside, they have together become corrupt; There is none who does good, No, not one.* (The New King James Version 1982)

God did not choose to wait for the world to come to Him; He made the first move and came to the world. Even while people mocked Him on the cross, He could cry out, "Father, forgive them." Even though they wanted Him dead, He wanted them saved.

The days of Church passivity are over. The Church must now become proactive in evangelism. Just as God took the initiative to save the lost world, so the Church must too take initiative in reaching lost souls. If saving lost souls is the heart of the Father, the Church needs to reflect that love.

Keeping His Own

God is just as passionate about keeping the lost as He is with saving them. *"The LORD shall preserve you from all evil; He shall preserve your soul."*

Psalm 121:7 (The New King James Version 1982). Once a person experiences salvation, God does not put them in the world and hope they will survive. He becomes involved very passionately with developing their character and helping them to overcome sin and life controlling habits.

Jesus passionately prayed for His followers in John 17; He prayed, *"While I was with them in the world, I kept them in Your name. Those whom You gave me I have kept; and none of them is lost except the son of perdition, that the Scripture might be fulfilled. ¹⁵I do not pray that You should take them out of the world, but that You should keep them from the evil one"* (John 17:12, 15) (The New King James Version 1982). "The Lord did **not pray** the Father **should take** believers home to heaven immediately; they must be left here to grow in grace and to witness for Christ. **But** Christ's prayer was they might be kept **from the evil one**. Not escape, but preservation." (MACDONALD 1990)

The ministries of the Church need to reflect this aspect of God's character. Concern for the well-being of Christian's is both God's heart and His will for the Church. Do you have a passion for the backslidden in heart? Do you care about the believer who disconnects from Church life? Indifference to their condition is a sin that needs to be repented of.

Task oriented people have the tendency to "move on" forgetting those who are falling behind. This attitude is heartless. People oriented individuals may allow anything to go so long as people remain in their Church. This is lukewarm compromise. The balance of these two will produce ministries that show compassion and concern and are proactive in restoring the dysfunctional and disruptive.

Chapter Nine

The Pastor

When you study Church growth and ministry effectiveness, you have to include a study on the Pastor. Whether you refer to this person as Pastor or you have another term, this person is the key to success for the Church on earth. As the Pastor, Jesus works through them to lead His Church into His fullness and purposes.

The purpose of this chapter is to examine the relational side of the Pastor as well as the task-oriented side. The principles shared here are effective for every level of ministry activity and therefore should be considered by all as pertinent and timely.

In chapter five, we discussed the character of God in the context of His interest in people. The Pastor must reflect this characteristic as well. If not, the chances are slim you will be an evangelistic, soul winning Church.

Before ministers of God can be effective in ministering to the needs of others, they must first minister to themselves. This is done through spiritual and academic development. Paul admonished Timothy to study the Scriptures diligently *"Be diligent to present yourself approved to God, a worker who does not need to be ashamed, rightly dividing the word of truth"* (2 Timothy 2:15) (The New King James Version 1982). "This latter expression means to handle the Scriptures correctly, to "hew the line," or as Alford put it, "to manage rightly to treat truth fully without falsifying."

(MACDONALD 1990)

Successful pastors are those that understand they never stop learning. Formal education may have a time limit based on levels of achievement, but once the academic classroom has fulfilled its purpose, the world becomes the classroom and the greatest teacher in the earth, the Holy Spirit, brings experience for understanding and new lessons for further learning.

The Task's of the Pastor

The task of the pastor is to make known the agenda of God in the earth. Jesus told His disciples to pray "Thy Kingdom come, Thy will be done, on earth as it is in heaven." I have found the number one issue for people seeking to serve God is they do not know His will for their life. It becomes necessary for leaders to know the written will of God and teach it in a way everyone can clearly grasp and fulfill. As the Church endeavors to fulfill the revealed will of God from the Scriptures, the will of God for their particular community will become evident.

There are not any short cuts that can be taken when it comes to the work of the Church. Jesus needs laborers in His harvest field because, quite honestly, it requires hard work to tend to the harvest field. Souls will not be won while everyone lounges at the banquet table and discusses all of the wonderful things God is going to do. Pastor's must initiate work and lead others to tending to the tasks. *Luke 10:2 (NKJV) [2] Then He said to them, "The harvest truly is great, but the laborers are few; therefore pray the Lord of the harvest to send out laborers into His harvest.* (The New King James Version 1982)

Every Church is "blessed" with philosophers, dreamers and observers, but what it needs more than these is laborers. A laborer primarily takes on the task of a servant. As such, he goes where the Master instructs him to go. It will take years of faithful work to bring about the full impact that a Church is capable of achieving, so be faithful and obedient.

In addition to working hard, a Pastor has to know how to work wisely. The labor of the minister must be connected to faith. Faith without works cannot be called faith. Faith without works is dead, and a dead faith is worse than no faith at all. Faith must work; it must bring into being; it must be observable. Spoken faith is not enough; cerebral faith is inadequate. Faith must be there, but it must be more. It must inspire action. True faith must manifest itself in works of faith.

Faith displays itself in works. Faith is more than mere words; it is more than knowledge; it is demonstrated by obedience; and it overtly responds to the promises of God.

Believe that God can and will work through you. As you begin to see fruit from your labors and faith, you will gain confidence and assurance. You may begin by believing for small things but soon your faith will rise up and go after bigger mountains and giants.

Wisdom demands Pastors carefully manage their priorities. Do not let the tyranny of the urgent determine what you will do from day to day. Know your mission and keep focused on God's agenda for you personally. There will always be voices crying for you to stop building your ministry and focus on them. When that does not work, do not be surprised if they start threatening you. Nehemiah faced these situations but sought wisdom from God and kept the Israelites focused on the task of rebuilding the wall.

Personal Development

The last and greatest task I want to share is that of personal development. The pressures a Pastor faces are hard to describe but without them a pastor will never become as His Savior in character or conduct. It is a given if you are in ministry, you are going to face pressure. Pressure comes from many different sources and comes in different degrees. It can either make you or break you. If you cannot handle pressure, the ministry is probably not the place for you.

Pressure can be a good thing. Every time I think of pressure, my mind travels back to my grandmother's kitchen. She used a pressure cooker to make an old-fashioned New England Dinner. She placed the vegetables and beef in a pressure cooker and placed it on the stove. When she turned up the heat, steam pressure began to build up in the sealed kettle. A small pressure release valve would allow a little pressure to be released so the kettle would not blow.

The reward from the pressure cooker was a meal where the flavors were deliciously blended and the meat was extremely tender. The pressure accomplished its goal. On the other hand, pressure can be destructive if there is not an outlet for it. This is perhaps one of the most destructive forces working against ministers.

So, how can we handle pressure without it destroying us? Can we turn a seemingly negative situation into a positive, productive experience? I believe we can. James said, *"My brethren, count it all joy when you fall into various trials, knowing that the testing of your faith produces patience. But let patience have its perfect work, that you may be perfect and complete, lacking nothing."* (James 1:2–4) (The New King James Version 1982). "Don't rebel! Do not faint! Rejoice! These problems are not enemies, bent on destroying you. They are friends which have come to aid you to develop Christian character" (MACDONALD 1990). By fighting and rebelling against the trials God ordains for us, we actually defeat ourselves and miss the opportunity to be precisely developed according to God's perfect plan.

Either pressure will drive you toward your goal or it will drive you away. Timidity is not a characteristic that will enable you to keep moving forward. You must face the challenge ahead of you with confidence in the Lord's ability to help you. Timothy fought with timidity in his life and it began to be detrimental to his ministry in Ephesus. Pastor's that do not develop courage in place of timidity should question either their calling or their willingness to obey Jesus. Paul told Timothy, *"For God has not given us a spirit of fear, but of power and of love and of a sound mind"* (2 Timothy 1:7) (The New King James Version 1982). The fact is many of us need a bit of encouragement from time to time to fan the flame of faith, which can so easily lose its glow and vitality with the course of time. To rekindle it, we need to give more thought to prayer, to the reading of God's Word, and to customary worship with God's people. We are not alone in this; we have the Holy Spirit who brings power, love and self-discipline.

Grow in wisdom and knowledge daily. Build your spirit through daily prayer and regular seasons of fasting. The more effective you are in personal development, the more you will be in developing the Disciples of Christ in your own ministry.

Reading For Inspiration and Information

"According to statistics compiled by The Literacy Co., 46% of American adults cannot understand the label on their prescription medicine." *(Copyright © 1996-2008 The Literacy Company, Inc. All Rights Reserved. Patents Pending.)*

"Students who reported having all four types of reading materials (books, magazines, newspapers, encyclopedias) in their home scored, on average, higher than those who reported having fewer reading materials." *(The Nation's Report Card: Fourth-Grade Reading 2000, April 2001, The National Center for Education Statistics).*

It is difficult to emphasize the importance of reading. There is a wealth of information available to us in book form. God has blessed authors with insight and ability to convey it in a way that helps us to grow.

In a class of 20 students, few if any teachers can find even five minutes of time in a day to devote to reading with each student.

As a part of our opening exercise at our Academy, I spend time reading to the students from good Christian literature. In addition, we have Christian literature available for them to read. We require them to spend at least 20 minutes each day reading. As hard as it may be, it is an essential part of their education.

People wonder, "Why do I have to read? I finished school and I don't want to do it anymore." Do you want to advance in your field or ministry? Do you want to excel in knowledge? If you answer yes to these questions, it is imperative that you become a reader.

Because of our unwillingness to read, we have in essence "dummed down" America. Illiteracy has become a plague to our nation as well as the Church. Fifty percent of American adults are unable to read an eighth grade level book. (Reading Statistic Reference Information, Jonathan Kozol, Illiterate America)

Do you want to see the Church go back to the Dark Ages? Ignorance and illiteracy kept Church-going people in bondage for centuries. They were at the mercy of ruthless, cutthroat, greedy Church leaders who manipulated people and used them for their own gain.

Today, ignorance to the Truth has many American Christians following deceptive spirits and doctrines of demons (1Tim 4:1-2). Reading the Bible and good, solid Christian literature will raise you to a higher level of understanding.

What is Man Compared to God?

Psalm 56:3-4 (NKJV) Whenever I am afraid, I will trust in You. ⁴ In God (I will praise His word), In God I have put my trust; I will not fear. What can flesh do to me? (The New King James Version 1982). In an act of arrogance, David's enemies were attacking him and continuously plotting his destruction. They began to join in an allied front to destroy David. With everything they had in them, they wanted to be rid of the man who had so utterly defeated them. They failed to recognize that David's victories were a result of the divine intervention of God on behalf of David and the nation he represented.

In the midst of the gloom and pressure, David's faith breaks forth in praise of God whom he has placed his trust. David has now gained a new perspective on his situation. Now, stress and fear will be turned to victory because he sees God who is bigger than his problem! David gained the understanding though he was the object of scorn and contempt, it was actually God the nations were rebelling against. Because of this, he was able to break out in praise because God is a vindicator of those that put their trust in Him *"What then shall we say to these things? If God is for us, who can be against us?"* (Romans 8:31) and *"Beloved, do not avenge yourselves, but rather give place to wrath; for it is written, "Vengeance is Mine, I will repay," says the Lord."* (Romans 12:19) (The New King James Version 1982)

Nothing can break through the hedge of protection God places around His servants, except it be allowed by God Himself. Then, God is still in control and will use the situation to strengthen you in your spirit. God had placed a hedge of protection around Job and his household. No damage could come to him unless the Lord allowed it. Believers today should take great comfort from the biblical teaching that the Lord protects His people.

David yielded to God under pressure and it transformed him into the leader that Israel needed.

King Herod yielded to pressure

Matthew 14:6-11 (NKJV) *⁶ But when Herod's birthday was celebrated, the daughter of Herodias danced before them and pleased Herod. ⁷ Therefore he promised with an oath to give her whatever she might ask. ⁸ So she, having been prompted by her mother, said, "Give me John the Baptist's head here on a platter." ⁹ And the king was sorry; nevertheless, because of the oaths and because of those who sat with him, he commanded it to be given to her. ¹⁰ So he sent and had John beheaded in prison. ¹¹ And his head was brought on a platter and given to the girl, and she brought it to her mother.* (The New King James Version 1982)

Moved by lust and pride, Herod made a promise he was not ready to keep. In order to save face, he had to have John, the prophet of God, beheaded. Herod knew he was playing with fire, but he bowed to the pressure of a young seductress. Herod stands as an example of terrible leadership. He is moved by his fleshly desires and arrogance. For him, it is all about appearance and there is no substance.

"Death, the temporary end of physical life, is not the worst enemy of humanity. Alienation from God is. And thus those who murdered John are far more pitiable than is John himself."

Keep Your Head in all Situations

2 Timothy 4:5 (NKJV) ⁵ But you be watchful in all things, endure afflictions, do the work of an evangelist, fulfill your ministry. (The New King James Version 1982) As the opposition to Timothy mounted, more than ever he was going to have to keep his head and be alert of the plots against him. He had to be on the alert and still preach the Gospel as if his life depended on it.

As it was with Timothy, so it is with us. We must faithfully fulfill the ministry God has called us to. Do not give your enemy the satisfaction of knowing he has defeated you. Be bold in the face of opposition and pressure, and with self-control, push forward to victory!

The Pastor and Relationships

A Pastor who is only task oriented most likely will crush the people following him. To a task-oriented pastor, people become a burden and a nuisance. To be effective, you must build a relationship with God and other people.

One of the scary aspects of ministry is being transparent before those you lead. If you develop your relationship with God properly, your inner, private life will be a thing that is worth sharing with others. Always remember, Pastors bleed, cry, hunger, thirst, and have bad days. By being open and honest, you will help others handle their problems in a God-honoring way.

People need to know you are approachable and touchable. Jesus calls to all those that hunger and thirst to come unto Him. As His ambassadors on earth, we must be available. This of course has to be balanced. Even Jesus knew when to withdraw from the crowds and find a place of solitude. After a forceful public confrontation with the Jewish authorities, Jesus withdrew to rest and to instruct His own disciples *"But Jesus withdrew with His disciples to the sea. And a great multitude from Galilee followed Him, and from Judea"* (Mark 3:7) (The New King James Version 1982)

Your mental and spiritual health is at stake. Be wise. Develop your personal relationship with God as well as with others. Tend to your work and you will be successful.

The Pastor is A Developer of People

A great Church does not happen overnight. It is built one person at a time. All people are a work in progress for a lifetime. By understanding this, you can develop a longsuffering attitude towards even the most dysfunctional person. The day will come when they will be ready to contribute to your ministry. In the meantime, realize the time you spend training them in character and gifts will eventually pay dividends.

Jesus demonstrated this kind of patience in developing the "character" of those He picked along the way. I often wonder what it must have been like for Him when He would teach and demonstrate, yet the disciples still did not get it. He talked about humility and they fought over titles and positions of prominence in the coming kingdom. Even through all of this, He did not give up on them. It took Him approximately three years to get them to the place they could actually understand. Do we owe any less to those we are working with?

Wise Pastor's develop developers. If you want to multiply your efforts, develop people into capable, reliable trainers. Release them to train and you will see your Church multiply and become a powerful influence in your community.

 Is It a Job or a Ministry?

A job is one you choose;

A ministry is one Christ chooses for you.

A job depends on your abilities;

A ministry depends on your availability to God.

In a job, you expect to receive;

In a ministry, you expect to give.

A job done well brings you self-esteem;

A ministry done well brings honor to Jesus Christ.

In a job, you give something to get something;

> *In a ministry, you return something that has already been given to you.*

A job well done has temporal remuneration;

A ministry well done brings eternal rewards. (Anonymous)

Chapter Ten

The Ministry of the Saints

Equipped by Church Leadership

Equipping means preparing, mending or restoring people to their original purpose. When the Church turned to professional ministers and took service away from the body, it deteriorated into an ecclesiastical nightmare. The body no longer was caring for itself thus causing stunted growth.

The requirements religious organizations have implemented have has created pride, prejudice and power struggles. Instead of moving forward, building the kingdom of God, organizations have reverted to politics in an effort to protect their prestigious positions of power. This sounds similar to the Pharisees and other religious leaders during Jesus' time.

Now, instead of Christians involving themselves in the activities of Jesus' Church, they stay in the shadows, feeling unworthy. "Without proper credentials, how can we serve? I haven't been to a seminary or college." people say. While these institutions can be used by God to equip, the ultimate responsibility for equipping the saints falls squarely on the shoulders of local Church leadership.

Always remember, a soul saved is a soul saved! If they are led to Christ through a seminary trained Christian or by a Church trained Christian, makes no difference to God. So, why does it to us?

Remember, equipping means preparing, mending or restoring people to their original purpose *"And He Himself gave some to be apostles, some prophets, some evangelists, and some pastors and teachers, for the equipping of the saints for the work of ministry, for the edifying of the body of Christ,"* (Ephesians 4:11–12) (The New King James Version 1982) This requires study of the Scriptures for the revelation of the purposes of the Saints.

The Ministry of Restoration

I believe one of the greatest tests of genuine leadership is restoring fallen leaders. The chances are high that if you are in leadership for any length of time you will either directly or indirectly be involved with the restoration of a fallen leader or fellow Christian. The important thing is to aim for restoration at all costs.

In our nation and in many places around the world, people have lost their moral compass. Values are shifting and now, that which is good is called bad and that which is bad, acceptable. The Apostle Paul said*, "Who, knowing the righteous judgment of God, that those who practice such things are deserving of death, not only do the same but also approve of those who practice them." (Romans 1:32,)* (The New King James Version 1982)

This shift towards immorality has exposed many dangers for the Christian and especially for the Christian leader. The answer, of course, is to rely on the grace of God and the power of His Spirit to be able to resist.

There is a great tension created by different religious backgrounds that range from pretending nothing happened to an unwillingness to ever trust a person and allow them to minister again. The Word of God is not silent on the issue. Consider the following passage carefully: *"Brethren, if a man is overtaken in any trespass, you who are spiritual restore such a one in a*

spirit of gentleness, considering yourself lest you also be tempted."
(Galatians 6:1,) (The New King James Version 1982)

First, Paul says, "any trespass." Yes, this includes all of the sins you can think of. Every individual must be dealt with according to what he or she has done and are at emotionally and spiritually. The process of restoration varies from person to person. There is not an industry standard to follow. Every situation needs to be handled with love, gentleness and much prayer.

Second, do not be like the Pharisee that was full of pride thanking God he was not a sinner like the publican. Every one of us is susceptible to falling into sin. *"Therefore let him who thinks he stands take heed lest he fall."* (1 Corinthians 10:12, (The New King James Version 1982) When you say, "I would never do that!" you are inviting a battle. The only way we stand is by the grace of God. The same grace that keeps us is the same grace that restores those who fall.

Another important scripture to apply in the ministry of reconciliation is from Proverbs 10:12, *"Hatred stirs up strife, But love covers all sins."* (The New King James Version 1982) We must not allow another person's failures to come between us. Love exhibits a willingness to move forward when there has been true repentance. *"A heart of love draws a curtain of secrecy over the faults and failures of others. These faults and failures must, of course, be confessed and forsaken, but love does not gossip about them or keep the pot boiling."* (MACDONALD 1990)

As a part of our ministry to the Saints, we must consider restoration as an essential ministry. We should have a basic plan of restoration in place even before the need arises.

The Sequence

There is a Biblical sequence when it comes to the ministry of the Saints. First, the "gifts" Apostles, Prophets, Evangelist's, Pastor's and Teacher's, equip the Saints for ministry; second, the Saints "do" the work of ministry;

third, the body is built up and functions properly.

Church growth is dependent upon the entire body, not just a few paid staff members. If the Church is not growing, examine the entire body, not just the Pastor. Church life and Church growth may begin with the Pastor, but it definitely does not stop there.

It takes a deliberate effort to bring the Church to maturity. Some growth may occur accidently, but it will not be of a significant amount. Maturity requires interaction and impartation. Reminders of the responsibilities of each member and opportunities must occur frequently. Remember, the first century Church met daily!

Meaningful Service

The Leadership of any Church must allow believers to participate in meaningful acts of service. When people begin to experience the joy of service, many of the interpersonal conflicts seemingly disappear. Depression and discouragement begin to fade away as people give of themselves to the cause of Christ.

There is a fear that people will fail. "Why should I let someone else do it if I can do it better?" is a question often asked as an excuse to hold on to ministry positions. Remember, a part of ministry training is to allow people an opportunity to make mistakes and then work with them to discover why they failed and help them to learn and move on. No one is perfect at the start, so please allow him or her to start.

Your Body is a Temple of the Holy Spirit

1 Corinthians 3:16 (NKJV) 16 Do you not know that you are the temple of God and that the Spirit of God dwells in you? (The New King James Version

1982) Our bodies should be tools of the spirit. Our regenerated spirit man gives expression through the body. Because the body is also the dwelling place of the Holy Spirit, it needs to be cared for out of respect of God.

Our physical health is an important issue we must address as leaders. Though we will inevitably die, our spirit will not. Our influence on the earth is dependent upon having a body to work through. Too many preachers have died at an early age because they have not cared for their temple, as they should.

Extended periods of stress, long meetings, sleeplessness, eating fast foods, will take its toll. Even though our minds may be sharp, our failing bodies will hinder us from effectively expressing the character of God and fulfilling His will on earth. There is not anything super-spiritual about abusing our bodies. It does not earn us a greater reward; in fact, it may even be a sin depending on the severity.

God forgave us for not caring for His temple. Become a better steward of your physical body, and you will reap the reward of finishing the race on earth. The Bible is clear we are to take good care of our bodies and physical exercise is a vital necessity. Our goal in exercise should not be to develop the quality of our bodies so other people will notice and think highly of us. Rather, the goal of exercising should be to improve our physical health so we will possess more energy that can be devoted to spiritual goals.

What Influence Are You Manifesting?

You and I are either manifesting God's influence or Satan's influence. People who profess allegiance to Christ, but through selfishness and rebellion serve their flesh are actually working for the enemy of their very soul.

Remember an important principal; Satan does not always manifest as the monstrous creature he really is. He is a master of appearing as an angel of light to deceive the weak of mind and spirit. *(2 Corinthians 11:14 NKJV)*

14 And no wonder! For Satan himself transforms himself into an angel of light. (The New King James Version 1982)

As leaders, we are called upon to live a life that fully pleases Jesus Christ and manifests His power in the earth. We cannot demand that Christians yield to Christ if we are not doing it ourselves. We defeat Satan by manifesting righteousness as given to us by God the Father through Jesus Christ. The ultimate price of sin is death (Rom. 6:23).

The Tension

There is a tension between the realm of the earth and the realm of the spirit. Most Christians see only in the dimension of the earth. The tension is created by trying to lead people who only see the reality of sickness, disease, poverty, injustice and extreme worldliness in their midst.

When faith-filled Christians make strong prophetic declarations, they are often misunderstood, criticized and even mocked. While the average believer is willing to adjust to the spiritual climate, the powerful Christian leader is unwilling to accept the status quo.

What are we to do? Meet the people where they are at, and, through strong teaching, preaching and demonstration of the Spirit and power, bring them to a faith-filled experience. Words alone may not be enough to convince them; people need to see a presentation of what we are preaching.

Remember, our bodies are instruments that can be used to bring in either the power of God or the deception of Satan. The Church does not need leaders that are more professional; it needs Holy Spirit baptized warriors carrying the banner of Jesus Christ into battle setting the captives free from religious bondages and lies of the enemy.

Where do you stand?

Chapter Eleven

Organizing for Fulfillment

As I began this dissertation, I wrote about working to perpetuate Churches. In this chapter, I will discuss the need for and the importance of organization.

Many people who have never pastored a church are unaware of the administrative duties that must be performed. While the pastor and church may have a great vision for reaching the lost, without proper planning and execution, it will remain only a dream.

When God entrusts a pastor with vision for the Church He has placed Him in, the Pastor must then begin to pray and ask the Lord for His plan of execution. Sharing the vision is essential, but by default, the pastor must also lead. Building a team to accomplish the goals requires management and steps to follow. Without clear direction given by the pastor, it is not likely that much will be accomplished. In addition, by setting goals and giving direction, the pastor is able to measure the progress and determine if more needs to be done or if things need to be changed.

A Gift for the Church

Administration is a spiritual gift given to the Church. "And God has appointed these in the church: first apostles, second prophets, third teachers, after that miracles, then gifts of healings, helps, administrations, varieties of tongues." (1 Corinthians 12:28) (The New King James Version 1982) "There are many possible definitions or organization. This one is very simple and task oriented; "Organization is the arrangement of persons to get a job done."

A key person to add to the staff is an Administrative Assistant. This person should be able to carry out routine administrative duties daily. This releases the pastor to focus on the more critical aspects of the ministry. In addition, this person should have strong Christian character, be trustworthy and faithful, able to keep confidences that could potentially be detrimental to parishioners character.

Biblically, three key offices are used to maintain the Church; the Pastor, Elders and Deacons. Each fulfills a significant role. While talent is a plus, character is the rule. The Apostle Paul gives biblical requirements of character to Timothy.

The Pastor needs to maintain a gentle spirit while leading people to accomplish the vision of God for the Church. Patience will enable people to grow as they learn. Mistakes will be made, but a wise and gentle pastor will lead and allow people to learn from their mistakes.

The Nature of the Church

The true nature of the Church is that it is an organism, not an organization. An organism is a complex structure of mutually supporting and secondary elements whose relations and properties are largely determined by their function in the whole. The church, an organism, is a basic unit developed to carry on the activities of its life by means of parts separate in function but mutually dependent. Such an organism requires administration—*good* administration—if it is to be very effective. If the objective becomes organization, the Church will eventually die from strangulation. The Churches survival depends upon keeping the organism organized.

All programs in the church are a part of the congregational program. It is important for the pastor to communicate this essential view. Without proper oversight and effective communication, these organizations can begin to act like separate entities.

More often than not, this dissension and separation is caused by a failure to exercise Scriptural oversight. The responsibility falls on the shoulders of the pastor and elder's. It is a natural tendency for people to pull away or drift away without oversight. There is a saying that sums this up: "you have to inspect what you expect."

It is essential the pastor and the elders function together in the oversight of the organizations to avoid this unfortunate dilemma. Simply having leaders of each organization give reports is not enough; the pastor needs to be more involved. While it is not necessary for him to attend every function, he can make himself available for consultation and troubleshooting. By occasionally attending the meetings associated with the organizations, his presence alone will let the groups and their leaders know he is concerned and is seeking their success.

While there are several practices the pastor may employ in keeping the organization running smoothly, most effective is showing appreciation to those involved in the congregational ministries.

The administrative department would be responsible to support all of the departments and their sub-ministries. The responsibilities should include, but not be limited to, financial management, budget management, business operations, building maintenance and management, and personnel management.

The common factor, which weaves through all the administrative functions, is the nature of the functions is *leading*. An administrator employs certain skills, techniques, and knowledge working in the privacy of his or her own thoughts and singular efforts. However, one does not become an administrator until they have related in a leadership way to the church or to a part of the church. One administers in relation to people, not things. The work of the administrator is chiefly leading and guiding persons.

Benefits of Effective Administration

There are at least four benefits a Church can derive from good administration. First, *the workload is distributed evenly.* Jethro told Moses, *"Both you and these people who are with you will surely wear yourselves out. For this thing is too much for you; you are not able to perform it by yourself."* (Exodus 18:18) (The New King James Version 1982) That certainly is true of ministry and the work of a church. No one person is big enough or good enough to do it all alone. There must be others to share the workload.

Second, *responsibility is distributed appropriately.* God has given a variety of gifts and each beneficiary is responsible for the best use of his or her gifts in relation to the church. With each person fulfilling his or her duty, the whole body can progress toward its goals.

Third, *good organization reduces confusion.* The workload is well distributed and the responsibility is placed where it belongs. Good job descriptions aid in the reduction of confusion and bring clarity to the task as well.

Fourth, *good organization helps avoid unnecessary doubling-up of effort.* Duplication of effort is at best a waste, and at worst counterproductive. Not only is time wasted, people become frustrated and can even feel a spirit of competition. This also is counterproductive.

The ultimate responsibility for the execution of administration belongs to the pastor. He may delegate responsibilities related to administration, but he is the chief administrator and unless he is involved with direct oversight, the chances of successful fulfillment are greatly diminished.

Bibliography

Adams, Jay E. *Shepherding God's Flock.* Grand Rapids: Zondervan, 1974, 1975.

Hybels, Bill. *Courageous Leadership.* Grand Rapids: Zondervan, 2009.

MACDONALD, WILLIAM. *Believer's Bible Commentary.* Nashville: THOMAS NELSON PUBLISHERS, 1990.

New Living Translation. Carol Stream: Tyndale House Publisers, Inc., 1996, 2004, 2007.

Peterson, Eugene H. *The Message (MSG) .* Colorado Springs: NavPress Publishing Group, Copyright © 1993, 1994, 1995, 1996, 2000, 2001, 2002.

Stowell, Joseph M. *Shepherding the Curch Into the 21st Century.* Victor Books/ SP Publications, 1994.

T.F. Zimmerman, G. Raymond Carlson, Zenas J. Bicket. *And He Gave Pastors.* Springfield: Gospel Publishing House, 1979.

The New King James Version. Nashville: Thomas Nelson, 1982.

Vine, W.E. *Vine's Complete Expository Dictionary Topic Finder.* Nashville: Thomas Nelson, 1997, c1996.

Warren, Dr. Rick. *The Purpose Driven Church.* Grand Rapids : Zondervan, 1995.

Warren, Rick. *The Purpose Driven Life.* Grand Rapids: Zondervan, 2002.

CPSIA information can be obtained
at www.ICGtesting.com
Printed in the USA
BVHW041145280421
606026BV00009B/118